KU-777-149

Cavalier King Charles Spaniels

SUSAN M. EWING

Project Team
Editor: Stephanie Fornino
Copy Editor: Joann Woy
Indexer: Lucie Haskins
Interior Design: Leah Lococo Ltd. and Stephanie Krautheim
Design Layout: Tilly Grassa
Cover Design: Angela Stanford

First published in United Kingdom 2008 by
Interpet Publishing
Vincent Lane
Dorking
Surrey
RH4 3YX

United Kingdom Editorial Team:
Hannah Turner
Nicola Parker

ISBN: 978 1 84286 175 2

Hampshire County Library	
C014386634	
Askews	Jul-2008
636.7 SPA	£8.99
	9781842861752

© 2008 by T.F.H. Publications, Inc.

All rights reserved. No part of this publication may be reproduced, stored, or transmitted in any form, or by any means electronic, mechanical or otherwise, without written permission from T.F.H. Publications, except where permitted by law. Requests for permission or further information should be directed to the above address.

Printed and bound in China

This book has been published with the intent to provide accurate and authoritative information in regard to the subject matter within. While every reasonable precaution has been taken in preparation of this book, the author and publisher expressly disclaim responsibility for any errors, omissions, or adverse effects arising from the use or application of the information contained herein. The techniques and suggestions are used at the reader's discretion and are not to be considered a substitute for veterinary care. If you suspect a medical problem consult your veterinarian.

INTERPET PUBLISHING

www.interpet.co.uk

Table of Contents

Chapter 1

Why I Adore My
Cavalier

All dog breeds are wonderful, but not every breed is right for every person. A Cavalier is not a watchdog, guard dog, or high-energy dog. If you jog long distances every morning in all weather and want a canine companion to join you, it won't be the Cavalier. The Cavalier King Charles Spaniel, as a breed, may have hunting ancestors, but today he's known as a lover, not a hunter.

History of the Cavalier

It's easy to trace the history of relatively modern dog breeds, but for breeds that have been around for hundreds of years, the early history may not exist. Also, hundreds of years ago, breeds didn't matter as much as what a dog could do. Good herding dogs, for example, were bred to other good herding dogs with the hope that the offspring would also be good herding dogs. The spaniel, as a type, has been around a long time, and the following is an educated guess as to how toy spaniels evolved.

Toy spaniels were developed in Great Britain to be hunters.

Hunter

Toy spaniels were developed in Great Britain, and their first function all those years ago was to be a hunter. King Canute (1016–1035) issued a decree that it was illegal to hunt with any dog who couldn't fit through a gauge 11 inches (27.9 cm) in diameter. Today, one can only wonder how such a dog could hold a stag or a boar, but maybe another category of dog was established for this type of hunting, or maybe this decree didn't stay in effect long. Whatever the answer,

the result of this decree was the development of a spaniel small enough to fit through that gauge. Modern-day Cavaliers are not considered hunting dogs, but some of them do retain a keen interest in birds and have a soft mouth, which means that they can pick up a bird without harming it.

Companion Dog

The rest of the Cavalier's heritage has been as a companion dog to the wealthy. Only the rich could afford to house a dog who didn't earn his keep as a hunter, guard dog, or ratter. At the court of Henry VIII (1509-1547), the only dogs allowed were "small spaniels for the ladies." In an age with no central heating, these small dogs were held on the lap for warmth—and to attract fleas away from their owner. The dogs also were placed under skirts to warm feet, and it was believed that they could cure stomach ailments. One of the names for these spaniels was "comforte dog."

In the 1600s, both King Charles I and King Charles II adored the breed, and it was from King Charles II, the "merry monarch," that the tiny dog received its name, Cavalier King Charles Spaniel.

The Modern-Day Cavalier

During the Victorian era (1837-1901), the toy spaniel was crossed with the Pug and Japanese Chin and became what is now called the King Charles Spaniel in Britain and the English Toy Spaniel in the United States.

In 1926, an American named Roswell Eldridge offered a cash prize at Cruft's dog show for anyone who entered a spaniel who looked like the spaniels in the old paintings. The money was tempting enough that

The Expert Knows

Law in Britain

There is a story that King Charles II of England (1660–1685) loved his dogs so much that he issued a decree that the King Charles Spaniel was to be allowed admittance into any public place, including the houses of Parliament. The story goes that this law is still on the books today. It's a wonderful story, but according to the Kennel Club, it's a myth.

several breeders worked to bring back the old style. This dog became the Cavalier King Charles Spaniel, to distinguish the breed from the King Charles Spaniel. The Cavalier is now the most popular toy breed in the United Kingdom.

Registry Recognition

The Cavalier King Charles Spaniel was recognised by Britain's Kennel Club in 1945. In January of 1996, the American Kennel Club (AKC) recognised the Cavalier.

In 1928 the Cavalier King Charles Spaniel Club was formed after a decision made by a group of exhibitors and breeders.

The first meeting was held on 3rd

Famous Cavalier Owners

If you have a Cavalier, you're in good company. Famous people who have owned Cavaliers include Lauren Bacall and Frank Sinatra. Former president Ronald Reagan had a Cavalier named Rex. Courteney Cox and David Arquette have Hopper and Harley. Princess Anastasia of Russia had a King Charles Spaniel named Jimmy, who died with the family, and a toy spaniel was at the side of King Charles I when he was beheaded. A Cavalier appeared on the cover of the February 24, 2006, edition of *Life*. Photographed by Chris Buck, the image is of an adorable tri-colour "reading" a book.

May 1929, which was the second day of Crufts that year.

Popularity of the Cavalier Today

The Cavalier has never had much public attention through appearances in movies or television, but he does fall in the top 20 of the most popular breeds and holds the number 6 position of the Kennel Club's breed registrations.

Physical Characteristics

What characteristics make the Cavalier the distinctive dog that he is today? Let's start by taking a look at some defining physical traits based on the breed standard. Keep in mind that this description is a reflection of the "ideal" Cavalier only; a dog who deviates from the breed standard can still make a wonderful pet.

Size

A Cavalier is larger than some toy dogs, but he is still a small dog. He should stand between 12 and 13 inches (30.5 and 33.0 cm) at the shoulders and should weigh between 12 and 18 pounds (5.9 and 8.1 kg). The Cavalier is slightly longer than tall.

Head

The Cavalier's head is slightly rounded but should look flat cross the top because the ears are set high. Those ears are long, with lots of "feathering" or fur, and when the dog is alert, the ears fan forward to frame the face. Cavaliers have black noses.

Eyes

The Cavalier's eyes set him apart from other breeds. They are large, round, and a warm, dark brown, giving him a very sweet expression.

Tail

Your Cavalier's tail will be wagging almost always, and that's as it should be. The tail should be in constant motion when the dog is in action.

Coat

The Cavalier's coat is of moderate length; it is silky and straight, with longer hair on the ears, chest, legs, and tail. A Cavalier's feet also are covered with this longer hair, which is a feature of the breed. If you don't plan to show your dog, a little trimming might make your Cavalier easier to keep clean and to groom.

Colour Patterns

Cavaliers come in four lovely colour patterns: Blenheim, tri-colour, black-and-tan, and ruby.

Blenheim

The most common colour is the Blenheim, which gets its name from the estate of the Duke of Marlborough. Marlborough's dogs were much desired for hunting, and all his dogs were chestnut and white. The chestnut markings are on a pearly white background, and the colour must cover both ears and eyes, with a white blaze between eyes and ears. In the centre of this blaze on the top of the head may be a spot of colour known as the "Blenheim spot." This spot is sometimes also called the "kissing spot."

The Cavalier has long feathered ears and soft brown eyes.

SENIOR DOG TIP

When Is My Cavalier a Senior?

You can expect your Cavalier to start slowing down a bit between the ages of eight and nine. You may not even notice any difference, but when your Cavalier turns eight, think about having your vet perform full blood screenings so that you can catch any problems early.

If your Cavalier wants to start taking life easy, don't push him. Your daily walks may have to be shorter, but as long as he's with you, he'll be happy.

Tri-Colour

Tri-colour Cavaliers have black markings on a pearly white background. As with the Blenheim, the colour should surround the ears and eyes, with a white blaze between the eyes. The dog should have tan markings over the eyes, on the cheeks, inside the ears, and on the underside of the tail.

Black-and-Tan

Black-and-tans are a jet black all over, with tan markings over the eyes, on the cheeks, inside the ears, and on the chest, legs, and the underside of the tail.

Ruby

Ruby Cavaliers are a rich red colour over their entire body.

Living With Your Cavalier

The Cavalier should be friendly and nonaggressive, never nervous or shy. Some of these traits are influenced by how well a dog is socialised. The more people your puppy meets, and the more strange places he's taken, the more friendly and stable his temperament will be.

Companionability

This endearing dog wants nothing more than to be with people, especially if one of those people is offering a warm, soft lap! That doesn't mean that a Cavalier won't enjoy the show ring with you, or that he can't do agility or obedience—it just means that he wants to be as close to you as he can get. As long as he can be with you, he's happy.

With Children

Cavaliers are wonderful with children in that they are small and gentle. There is a danger, however, of a child harming this small, delicate dog. Very young children may not fully understand the need to be gentle with a Cavalier, and many breeders recommend that children be at least seven years old

Cavaliers usually adjust well to other pets, including cats.

before a Cavalier joins the family.

Make sure that all children understand the need to be gentle. Supervise younger children, who may be inclined to pull a tail or an ear, or who might want to wrestle with the dog. Cavaliers might be willing to play rough, but they are just too small for those kinds of games.

With Other Pets

Cavaliers like to be single dogs, but they adjust well to other pets. One way to help to ensure harmony is to get a second dog of the opposite sex. It also helps if the new dog is younger than the established pet so that he is more willing to be submissive. Introduce the dogs in a neutral area, and keep them on slack leads until you're sure they will get along. Feed them separately to prevent arguments over food, and put some distance between their beds so that there's no squabble over who sleeps where.

If you have a cat, make sure that she always has a way to escape from the dog. Clear a shelf in a room so that the cat can get up high, or put a baby gate across a doorway. Cats can generally leap in and out of a room over these gates, leaving the dog behind.

Your Cavalier may even become friends with smaller pets, like rabbits, guinea pigs, hamsters, or gerbils, but don't count on it. Dogs tend to consider small, rapidly moving, squeaking animals as prey. Keep your

FAMILY-FRIENDLY TIP

Cavaliers and Children

Cavaliers are loving, playful dogs, but they are also small and can be injured with rough play. Limit long hikes, lots of jumping, or roughhousing until their growth plates are fully closed at around eight to nine months. For this reason, many breeders refuse to sell a Cavalier to a family with very small children, preferring their puppies to go to homes where the children are seven years old or older. One breeder discourages families from owning a Cavalier if they have children under the age of five.

A Cavalier will never be the ideal teammate in a game of football, but for older children who understand the fragile nature of a toy dog, the Cavalier will be a loving companion. Remember to make proper introductions and to supervise play with younger children. Any dog, even a Cavalier, can snap if he is afraid or hurt.

small pets safely caged, and keep the cage out of your dog's reach.

Environment

The Cavalier doesn't care where he lives as long as he can be with his people. He doesn't need the wide open spaces of rural living, but although he doesn't need much space, he can certainly enjoy a romp in a field if his family enjoys country living. Life in the suburbs is fine, too, if it includes a bit of garden or daily walks down the road. The Cavalier is also delighted to share an urban flat or apartment. Give him his daily walk, or train him to paper or a litter box (see Chapter 6), and your Cavalier will be a contented city dweller.

Exercise Requirements

Schedule some exercise for your dog each day. A Cavalier will be perfectly willing to spend his entire life in a lap or snuggling on the sofa, but that kind of life isn't good for anyone. Run around the garden, throw a ball, or take your darling for a brisk walk around the neighbourhood. You can't expect your Cavalier to run a marathon, but he should still get exercise.

Cavaliers are definitely housedogs. They don't mind a romp in the snow, but they were not bred to curl up in a snowdrift for a nap and certainly should never be left outdoors for hours at a time.

Trainability

If you're looking for a dog to earn that perfect score in obedience, the Cavalier is probably not the breed for you. Cavaliers were bred to be companion dogs. There was never any demand on them to do anything other than be charming pets. That doesn't mean that you can't train them, but it does mean that they don't have that built-in desire to obey or to work at a job. Being cute is their job.

Sometimes people don't bother training small dogs just because they are small—they can be picked up if they're noisy or in the way. Also, small dogs don't pose much of a threat. If a Cavalier jumps up, for example, he's not likely to knock a person down. This doesn't mean that small dogs shouldn't be trained, though. All dogs should be well behaved, including your Cavalier.

Remember that you are dealing with a small dog, so when training, don't overwhelm him with your size or with a loud voice. Be firm, but be quiet about it. Use positive reinforcement and

patience, and keep your training sessions short.

Watchdog? It's doubtful. Hunter? Not anymore. Lover? Now you're talking. The Cavalier is a bright, cheerful dog who's happiest when he's with his family, and if he can curl up in your lap and give your chin a lick now and then, his life is complete.

Modern-day Cavaliers are bred to be companion dogs only, which means that they don't have a built-in desire to obey.

Chapter 2

The Stuff of
Everyday Life

It's time to go shopping! Your new puppy will need his own bed, collar, food and water dishes, grooming supplies, lead, and toys, and shopping for these items is almost as much fun as choosing the right dog in the first place.

Bed

You'll want your new friend to have a cosy bed, but it might be a good idea to wait until your dog is a bit older before you invest in an expensive one. Young dogs can have housetraining accidents, and they also may think that their bed makes a great chew toy.

To construct a doggy bed yourself, use old bath towels or bits of artificial fleece. These can make a warm, soft bed but are also easily washed. If they get chewed, at least it's an old towel and not an expensive innerspring mattress!

Collar

A lightweight collar will do just fine for your toy breed. While your Cavalier is growing, consider a soft, flat buckle collar that allows you to push the buckle tongue through the fabric at

any point. With this type of collar, the collar grows with the dog.

Once your dog is fully grown, consider a permanent flat buckle collar. Soft, rolled leather is a nice choice, but many nylon collars in assorted colours are available too. You can colour coordinate your collar and lead if you select nylon.

No matter what kind of collar you choose, make sure that it fits properly. You should be able to fit two fingers between your dog's neck and the collar.

Harness

A harness is another option, but be aware that you don't have as much control with a harness, and it may encourage your dog to pull.

Crate

Many people look at a crate and think "jail," but you must look at a crate from your dog's point of view. A dog is a den animal who appreciates a cosy, safe place to curl up for a nap. That's what a crate becomes. Many dogs go into their crates on their own for naps and sleep in them at night, even with the door wide open. Think "den" and you're on the right track.

Crate Benefits

A crate may seem expensive, but it will last for the life of your dog

You should be able to fit two fingers between your dog's neck and his collar.

and is worth it. A crate is a wonderful tool for housetraining your puppy, and it keeps him safe when you're not home to supervise his exploration. Crates also help to make travel easier and keep your dog safe when he's riding in the car.

Types of Crates

Crates come a variety of different materials, including plastic, wire, and soft sided.

Plastic

Plastic crates offer a cosy den but may hold in more heat in summer and are a bit harder to clean.

Wire

Wire crates generally have a removable tray that makes cleaning easier, and they provide more ventilation. The drawback is that they are not very den-like; you can remedy that by draping a blanket or towel over the crate. In hot weather, just remove the covering for instant ventilation.

Soft Sided

Soft-sided crates fold easily and are useful for travelling. They're much easier to carry into a hotel room than is a regular crate.

Crate Fit

Choose a crate that fits your dog. He should be able to lie down, stand up, and turn around in it. If the crate is too big, your dog may use one end as a

The Expert Knows

Identification

The Control of Dogs Order 1992 stipulates that any dog in a public place must wear a collar with an ID tag showing the name and address of the owner. You could face a fine of up to £5,000 if you do not comply.

bedroom and the other end as a bathroom, which will slow down the housetraining process.

Crate Cautions

As wonderful as a crate is, it can be abused. A crate is not meant to be a substitute for owner care. Your Cavalier needs lots of attention, and should be with you whenever possible. Use the crate as a housetraining tool and to keep your dog safe when you're away from home, but don't keep him crated all the time.

Exercise Pen

With an exercise pen (or x-pen for short), you can block off a portion of a room, keeping your puppy confined in the designated area. An x-pen is also useful when you want your puppy to enjoy a little outdoor freedom but there's no safe fenced area. If you travel a lot or plan to attend organised dog events, an x-pen is a good investment.

Food and Water Dishes

Your Cavalier needs his very own food and water dishes, and lots of choices are available, including stainless steel, ceramic, and plastic. Whatever type of dish you choose, make sure that you keep the dishes clean. Water dishes must be washed regularly, even though they only hold water. Refill the dish with fresh, clean water. Wash your dog's food dish as well. If you decide to free feed—leaving food out and available to your dog all day—start each day with fresh food and a clean dish.

Stainless Steel

Stainless steel is one of the best options. It is practically indestructible and easy to clean. Some stainless steel bowls have a rubber bottom to prevent them from being pushed across the floor.

Ceramic

Ceramic bowls often come with attractive designs or cute sayings, and they are usually too heavy for a Cavalier to tip over. One drawback is that they can break. If you choose this type of bowl, make sure that the glaze is lead-free.

Plastic

Plastic bowls have the advantage of being unbreakable, but they can be hard to get clean (tiny cracks in the plastic can harbour bacteria), and some dogs may get acne on their chins from rubbing their faces on the plastic.

Gate

Use a doorway gate to keep your puppy in the kitchen or other puppy-proof room, or use a gate to bar him from exploring the living room. A gate

Dogs are den animals who appreciate the security that a crate provides.

Setting Up a Schedule

Dogs are creatures of habit who do well with a structured routine. Set times for feeding, walking, and playing help your dog feel secure. At the same time, dogs are flexible. If you feed your dog twice a day, for example, the meals don't have to be evenly spaced. At my house, it works for me to feed my dogs at about 6:30 a.m. each morning and then again at 1:30 p.m. In addition, having a regular walk time helps your dog control his bladder. Your dog may not wear a watch, but he knows what time to expect a walk!

also can add a level of safety for the family cat. Most cats can jump easily over a gate, leaving the rambunctious puppy behind.

Grooming Supplies

Your Cavalier needs regular brushing to keep that silky coat clean and tangle-free. For bath time, use a shampoo especially made for dogs. Next, invest in a good pin brush and a comb. A pin brush has flexible bristles, each one topped with a tiny round ball. A Cavalier doesn't have a thick undercoat, so there's no need to buy brushes meant to loosen and remove that coat. If you like, you also may buy a slicker brush for combing the ears, but otherwise, a pin brush and comb will do nicely. Next, you'll need a pair of nail clippers. Nails that grow too long make it hard for a dog to walk, and the foot tends to spread as well.

Pay special attention to your dog's ears. Those long, silky ears are lovely, but they also prevent air circulation. Use an ear cleanser once a week or so, and check for any sign of irritation or infection.

If you aren't going to show your dog, you may want a small pair of sharp scissors to trim some of his foot fur. Cavaliers are shown untrimmed, but if your dog will be a pet only, trimming the foot fur will help keep him—and

A brush is an essential grooming supply that will keep your Cavalier's coat clean and tangle-free.

FAMILY-FRIENDLY TIP

Kids and Dog-Related Chores

A dog can be a wonderful companion for a child, and having dog-related chores can teach a child responsibility, but a child never should be a dog's sole caretaker. Choose age-appropriate jobs for your child, like changing the water in the water bowl or measuring the dog food. An older child may be able to walk a dog or brush him, but children can forget, and your dog shouldn't suffer because of it. It's up to you to make sure that your dog is properly fed, watered, and exercised, no matter what your children do. Health care is up to you too, as is proper training. It may be "the kids' dog," but he is your responsibility.

your home—cleaner, and there'll be less fur to collect burrs.

Identification

Your dog must have an ID tag attached to his collar. Put your telephone

Choose a nylon or leather lead for your Cavalier.

numbers on the tag so that if your dog is lost, the finder will be able to call you. Consider putting your dog's name on the tag, although some people worry that this will help a thief. If a person is close enough to read the tag, though, she already has your dog, so I don't think this should be a concern.

The problem with tags is that they can come off or be taken off, so you may want to consider a more permanent form of identification. Microchips—tiny electronic chips implanted between your dog's shoulder blades—provide a way to identify your dog, with no chance of the device being lost. Each chip contains your dog's individual number, registered with a specific tracking agency. A shelter worker or veterinarian can read the chip with a special scanner, contact the registration agency, and that agency will, in turn, contact you.

Lead

Leads come in various materials and lengths, but the best length for general walking and training is 6 feet (1.8 m). Choose nylon or leather, but stay away from chain. A chain lead will likely be too heavy for your Cavalier, and chain is hard on your hands if you hold it and your dog pulls.

Toys

Now that you've purchased the essentials, it's time to have some fun with toys. Dozens of types and shapes are available, and eventually you may discover that your dog prefers one kind to another. Until then, keep a couple of things in mind. One is the size of the toy— too big is better than too small. A toy that is too small can be swallowed and may either stick in your dog's throat or cause an obstruction in the intestines.

Another thing to remember is to supervise play, at least in the beginning. Latex squeaky toys can pose a threat if your dog shreds the toy and swallows the hard part that makes the noise. Some dogs never do this; others make it their mission in life to get to the noisemaker. The same is true of stuffed toys that have a noisemaker

SENIOR DOG TIP

Helping the Older Dog Adjust

Puppies quickly adapt to their surroundings, but an older dog may need a little help. If you're giving a home to an older dog, try to stick to whatever schedule he may have been used to. If you know when he was fed and walked, try to follow that schedule for the first few weeks. If he's always been allowed to sleep on the couch, think about whether you can cover your couch and allow him that same privilege. Keep him on the same food he's always had. If you make a change, make it gradual.

buried inside. I've had dogs who just enjoyed carrying the toy around, occasionally chewing on it. I've also had dogs who could rip open a stuffed toy in ten minutes in an effort to get to the squeaky. Until you know what your dog will do, supervise the play.

This chapter covers the basics, but you'll find many more items to buy in shops and catalogues. It's fine to pamper your Cavalier, but keep your dog's safety in mind.

Chapter 3

Good Eating

Most dogs enjoy eating, and many will eat just about anything. It's up to you to make sure that your dog eats the right foods. This chapter explores different foods and ways you can ensure that your dog gets a diet that helps to keep him healthy.

The Balanced Diet

Just like people, dogs need a balanced diet for proper growth and to stay healthy. Dogs require carbohydrates, fats, minerals and vitamins, proteins, and water, but they need them in different proportions from people. That's why feeding a dog "people food" all the time doesn't guarantee a balanced diet. Dogs need a high percentage of both fat and protein, and many people foods can be harmful to dogs. That luscious chocolate bar can be fatal to your dog. Ignore your dog's pleading looks, and keep the people food for people.

Carbohydrates

Carbohydrates provide energy and help with digestion. Simple carbohydrates quickly convert to glucose. Complex carbohydrates take longer to break down, and they provide a steady amount of energy. Plant products, such as grains, fruits, and vegetables, all provide carbohydrates.

Fats

No one wants an overweight dog, but that doesn't mean that fats aren't important in the diet. In addition to adding flavour, fats provide energy and help the body use fat-soluble vitamins like A, D, E, and K. A certain amount of body fat helps to store these vitamins and helps to prevent a vitamin deficiency. Oils provide fats, as do meats.

Minerals and Vitamins

Minerals and vitamins help to process carbohydrates, fats, and proteins, as well as help with other specific functions. For example, vitamin A helps with bone growth and also vision.

Always make clean, fresh water available to your Cavalier.

Reading Dog Food Labels

No matter what kind of food you choose, it's still up to you to choose the food that best meets your dog's needs, so read the label.

An animal-based protein should be one of the first five ingredients listed. Ideally, it should be one of the first three. Beef, chicken, turkey, and lamb are the usual types of meat listed. Don't be put off by "meat by-products." You might not want to eat them, but "by-products" include organ meats, and they can be a rich source of protein, vitamins, and minerals. The food should not contain hooves, horns, feathers, fur, or manure.

Preservatives, if any, also will be listed on the label. If you prefer a food with natural preservatives, buy smaller quantities to ensure freshness.

Check the label for added sugars. The label may list sugar, or it may say sucrose. These sugars are unnecessary and add empty calories to your dog's food. They're more likely to be found in semi-moist foods than in tinned or dry foods.

Vitamin K is essential for proper blood clotting. Minerals help with blood flow and healing. Calcium, phosphorus, and magnesium help to create bone. Minerals also are essential for the normal functioning of muscles and nerves, and aid in hormone production. Minerals and vitamins are found in varying amounts in all foods, and many commercial dog foods add vitamins and minerals that might otherwise be lacking, or that may have been destroyed during food processing.

Proteins

Protein is the "building block" for dogs, just as it is for people. Dogs need protein for growth, strong muscles, and a healthy coat and nails. Meat is a good source of protein, which is why it should be one of the first three ingredients in your dog's food. Meat is an excellent source of protein. Beef, chicken, and lamb are common sources of protein in dog food.

Water

Water is essential to life. Sixty to 70 percent of your dog's weight is water. Water is the main ingredient in the cells of the body, and it helps in digestion, removal of body wastes, and in regulating body temperature. It's a major component of saliva, and it helps to lubricate joints. Always have clean water available for your Cavalier.

Commercial Dog Foods

Commercial dog foods didn't become popular until after World War II. Before that, people fed table scraps and bones from the butcher. Today, supermarket shelves are loaded with dozens of brands of dog food, all nutritionally balanced. Being nutritionally balanced, however, doesn't mean that every food is right for every dog. Dogs can have food allergies, just like people. A food that is just right for one dog may be too rich or too low in protein for another dog. Some of the differences depend on the individual dog, and some differences may be a result of the particular dog's activity level. It's up to you to determine what is best for your dog.

What type of food you choose depends a lot on your particular

Cavalier. Initially, you may want to continue with whatever food your breeder recommends. Then, depending on availability and how well your dog does on the food, you may want to try something else. Whether you choose dry, semi-moist, or tinned, name-brand foods are your best choice because the formula is unlikely to see frequent changes. You'll know if you've made the right selection if your dog's coat is shiny and thick, he is energetic, and his eyes are clear and bright.

Dry Food (Kibble)

Dry food, or kibble, is the least expensive type of dog food. Depending on the speed with which your Cavalier eats his food, the crunchy texture may give him some chewing exercise and may help to clean his teeth. Dry food contains a protein source, such as beef, chicken, turkey, or lamb, and a filler grain. Corn is frequently used, but the grain may be wheat, rice, or soy. Generally, there will be added vitamins and a preservative. Natural preservatives break down faster than do synthetic preservatives, so if you like the idea of natural preservatives, remember that, because they break down faster, your food will spoil faster. You

Dry food, or kibble, may help to clean your Cavalier's teeth.

Feeding Chart

This chart offers a rough guideline for feeding your Cavalier from puppyhood through his senior years. Your dog may need more or less than the amounts listed, depending on how active he is and what brand of food you choose. Talk to your breeder and your veterinarian about what's best for your dog. Some breeders never feed puppy foods, and some senior dogs may do just fine on the adult food they've always eaten.

Age	Times per Day	Amount	Best Food
Puppies (up to 6 months)	2-3 depending on age	½ to ⅔ cup (118.3 to 157.7 ml) each feeding	Puppy or adult food
Adolescents (6 to 18 months)	2	¾ cup (177.4 ml) each feeding	Adult Food
Active adults (18 months to 7 years)	2	¾ to 1 cup (177.4 to to 236.6 ml), each feeding, depending on activity level	Adult Food
Sedentary adults (7 to 9 years)	2	⅓ to ⅔ cup (78.9 to 157.7 ml) each feeding	Adult or Senior Food
Seniors (9+ years)	2	⅓ to ⅔ cup (78.9 to 157.7 ml) each feeding	Adult or Senior Food

don't need to refrigerate dry food, but it can get stale, and depending on how much fat it contains, can turn rancid. Buy dry food in the smallest sized bag possible to help keep it fresh. You also can buy storage bins with airtight lids that help to keep food from spoiling.

If you decide to feed your Cavalier a dry food, choose one with a small kibble, designed for a smaller dog. It's not just the size of the kibble; smaller dogs have a different rate of metabolism than larger dogs and need a different type of food.

Semi-Moist Food

Semi-moist foods are generally more expensive than either dry or tinned foods. They don't need refrigeration, and as long as they stay packaged, they have a long shelf life. These foods frequently are moulded into patties or cute shapes, like drumsticks. They may be coloured to look like fresh ground beef or cheese.

Semi-moist foods are convenient because they tend to be packaged in individual serving sizes, and most dogs love them. However, they generally contain more sugar and flour than other forms of dog food. The sugar and flour help to keep the food moist and in the desired shape, but your dog doesn't need these extra empty calories. Semi-moist foods also can stick to teeth surfaces and could cause dental damage.

Tinned Food

Tinned foods fall somewhere in the middle between dry and semi-moist foods as far as price goes. They must be refrigerated after opening. Tinned foods have a major protein source and added vitamins and minerals; there may or may not be a grain filler. Tinned foods contain more water than other food types, and you'll need more of it to equal the calorie content of a serving of dry food. As a general rule, 1 ounce (28.3 g) of dry food has three and a half times the number of calories as 1 ounce (28.3 g) of tinned food.

Tinned food smells wonderful to your dog, even if it doesn't to you, so if you have a fussy eater, tinned food may encourage him to eat. Many people mix tinned and dry foods to tempt their dogs' appetites and stretch their budgets, and tinned food gives you a place to hide any medication your Cavalier might need.

Noncommercial Diets

Some people prefer to prepare their dogs' food themselves using fresh foods and either cooking or feeding raw. Both of these options take more time than just opening a tin or a bag, and you must make sure that your dog is still

Food Allergies

If your dog is biting or licking at his paws or his body, especially at the base of the tail, he may be allergic to something in his food. Check with your veterinarian to rule out any other causes, and then inspect the label of your dog food. If the main grain is corn, try a food with wheat or rice. If the main protein is chicken, switch to lamb. Try a food with lower fat or protein. If these changes don't eliminate the problem, talk to your veterinarian about a one-ingredient food, usually available from your vet. This is the beginning of a slow process of determining just what your dog is allergic to. When you switch foods, do so gradually over a period of four to five days to prevent digestive tract upsets.

getting a balanced diet. Feeding raw doesn't mean just throwing your Cavalier a bone, and cooking doesn't translate to table scraps. Your dog still needs the proper combination of carbohydrates, fats, proteins, minerals, and vitamins to stay healthy.

Talk to your breeder, your veterinarian, and other dog owners for ideas on what you should feed, but don't do anything that makes you uncomfortable. Both raw and home-cooked diets take time and effort. If you don't have time to cook for your dog, or don't feel comfortable trying to supply a balanced diet, then stick with a top-quality commercial food.

Keep in mind that, whether you decide to feed raw or home-cooked meals, you'll need to plan ahead if you go on a trip with your dog, or if you board him. Keep the food cold while travelling, and if you plan to board your dog, make sure that the kennel operator has a place to store your dog's food and is willing to feed according to your instructions.

BARF (Raw) Diet

BARF is an unfortunate acronym that stands for Bones and Raw Food, or Biologically Appropriate Raw Food. Dogs on the BARF diet eat raw, meaty bones, organ meat, muscle meat, and vegetables.

Raw feeding consists of one meal a day of raw, meaty bones and another meal that alternates between muscle meat, organ meat, and vegetables. Vegetables must be broken down in a blender or a food processor because dogs can't break down the cellulose in plants. You can feed your dog just about any vegetable he'll eat, but leave out the onions because they can cause haemolytic anaemia in dogs. When feeding muscle and organ meats, consider "dirty" tripe. This is tripe (stomach tissue) that still contains partially digested vegetable matter.

A nutritious diet will help to keep your Cavalier happy and healthy.

If you decide to feed raw, you'll need enough freezer space to store all the meat and bones. Most people who feed raw also cook up batches of the vegetable mix and freeze individual meal portions. If you have only one Cavalier, your regular refrigerator freezer may give you enough room.

Be prepared for a bit of controversy if you decide to feed your Cavalier a raw diet. Many veterinarians are against feeding raw meat because of the threat of both *Salmonella* and *Escherichia coli* bacteria in raw foods. Proponents of the raw diet say that their dogs have shinier coats, cleaner teeth, and fewer health problems. Some people grind the bones to eliminate any possibility of a problem from bone splinters. If you think that a raw diet is right for your dog, check with your veterinarian. She may recommend a blood test before you start the diet and then a re-test every six months to monitor your dog's health and make sure that he is getting the nutrition he needs.

Home-Cooked Diet

You may like the idea of steering away from commercial foods but may not want to feed raw because of concerns about bacteria. If that's the case,

The Expert Knows

Table Manners

Your dog won't need to know which fork is for salad or which spoon to use for the soup, but he'll need to learn some table manners all the same. Dogs are very food motivated, and they don't need much reinforcement to learn where and when they might get a handout. It's hard to resist the melting brown eyes of a Cavalier as he looks up at you while you're eating, but resist. Make it the family rule to never, ever feed the dog from the table, or that melting gaze will watch every bite you take for the next 12 years or so.

consider home cooking. As with a raw diet, you'll need to make sure that the diet is balanced.

With home cooking, as with raw feeding, you can alternate between a meat meal and a vegetable meal. Cooked vegetables mixed with oatmeal make a good base for a nonmeat meal. The meats you feed can be the same as when feeding raw, only you cook the meat. Cook ground beef, chicken, or turkey. Cook liver and chicken gizzards. The only exception is to never, ever give your dog cooked bones. Raw bones are softer and can be chewed up, but cooked bones can splinter and puncture your dog's intestines. Cooked bones are also harder and can crack or break your

Cavalier's teeth. One way to get the benefit of bones is to cook chicken legs in a slow cooker. Cover the chicken legs with water and cook on low for 24 hours. This turns the bones to mush, and your dog will love it.

As with feeding raw foods, plan to cook a large batch of food and then freeze individual portions to save time.

Supplements

A healthy dog eating a balanced diet shouldn't need supplements. However, if you're cooking for your dog, you may need to add supplements to make sure that your dog is getting all the nutrients he needs. Dogs with health concerns may also need supplements; for example, glucosamine may help a dog with arthritis. Talk to your veterinarian if you think that your dog needs a supplement.

Treats

Treats are any food that falls, literally and figuratively, outside your Cavalier's bowl. A treat can be a bite of turkey from the Christmas meal or a spoonful of vanilla ice cream on your dog's birthday. That bedtime dog biscuit is a treat, and you may be using treats to train your spaniel. Treats should make up no more than 10 percent of your dog's diet. Limit table scraps, break dog biscuits in half, and for training, cut up soft treats into itsy-bitsy pieces. Your Cavalier will

work just as hard for those tiny bits as he will for the entire, larger treat, and you'll be helping him watch his weight and eat right.

Feeding Schedules

Now that you've decided what to feed, the next question is how? There are two methods: free feeding and scheduled feeding.

Free Feeding

With free feeding, you measure out your dog's daily food allowance, and the food is available all day for the dog to munch on whenever he's hungry. With only one dog, free feeding may work well, but in a multiple-dog household, there's no way to know how much each individual dog is eating. The more dominant dog may

Treats should make up no more than 10 percent of your dog's diet.

FAMILY-FRIENDLY TIP

Children and Feeding Your Cavalier

Even very young children like to help to take care of the family dog, and feeding is one of the easiest chores. Depending on your child's age, she may be able to take over feeding completely. This means putting down a bowl of fresh water as well as the food. Make sure that there's a proper measuring scoop in the dry food so that the child can give the dog just what he needs. If you're feeding tinned food, older children can open tinss and scoop out food. Younger children may not be able to scoop or open tins, but if you put the food in the bowl, that youngster will be delighted to be the one to put the bowl in front of the dog.

Teach your child to give the *sit* command before she puts down the bowl. (For how to teach *sit*, see Chapter 6.) This not only teaches the dog to wait, but it prevents an eager dog from jumping up and knocking a child down. Also, make sure that your child understands that dinnertime is not playtime—never let her tease the dog with the food.

Remember that feeding the dog is ultimately your responsibility. Keep an eye on the situation and remind your child of her duties, or if necessary, feed the dog yourself.

be getting it all. If you are feeding anything but dry kibble, the food can attract bugs and flies, and there's a risk of the food spoiling. Another disadvantage of free feeding is that if your dog needs medication and you are mixing it with food, there's no way to time the dosage or to make sure that he eats it all at once.

Scheduled Feeding

With scheduled feeding, the food is put down at a regular time and the dish is picked up after 15 or 20 minutes. You know exactly how much food your dog

has consumed, so it's easier to control his weight. If your dog is under the weather and not eating, or eating less, you'll know right away. The food is always fresh with scheduled feeding.

How Much to Feed

You know what you're feeding, and when. The next question is how much? An overweight dog faces many of the same problems as an overweight human. The extra weight can contribute to joint stress, heart problems, and diabetes. Remember that the feeding suggestions on packaged food are just that—suggestions. Your dog may need more or less, depending on how active he is. You should be able to feel your dog's ribs, and he should have a definite waist—an indentation behind his ribs. If weight loss or gain is sudden, check with your veterinarian to make sure that no health problems are present. Otherwise, try not to let your dog pile on the extra pounds (kg).

Dealing With Obesity

It's hard to resist those amazing Cavalier eyes as he looks from your ice cream bowl to you, but harden your heart when it comes to extra snacks, especially people food. If your dog is overweight, put him on a diet. You control his food, and he can't sneak into the kitchen and raid the refrigerator at midnight. Cut back on portions. Try adding a bit of tinned pumpkin (not pumpkin pie mix) to help your dog feel full. If he is used to a dog biscuit at certain times of the day, break the biscuits in half. Your dog will be happy, and you will have saved a few calories.

Add a bit more exercise to the day. If your normal walk is three times around the park, make it four. If your dog has a canine friend, arrange a play date. If your Cavalier enjoys playing fetch, add another game or two to your routine. It won't be long before he is once again at his correct weight. A large part of keeping your dog

SENIOR DOG TIP

Feeding the Older Dog

Your senior Cavalier likely will need fewer calories as he ages, and senior foods are available that offer both fewer calories and less protein. Also, cut back on treats to cut calories. Your dog will expect his customary treats at their normal times, so break those biscuits in half, or cut soft treats into smaller pieces.

Check your senior's teeth. Cracked, worn teeth may make eating dry foods painful. A checkup at your veterinarian's, including a blood test, will help to determine if any health problems exist that may be helped with a specific diet. Your dog may need even less protein, or he may require a food that supplies more of a specific vitamin or mineral.

healthy is based on what you feed him.

He can't put himself on a diet or take supplements on his own to balance his diet. Take the time to read labels, pay attention to your dog's reaction to certain foods, and talk to your veterinarian about the best diet for your Cavalier.

Chapter 4

Looking Good

There's nothing cuter than a Cavalier, so you'll always want yours looking his best when admiring strangers stop to pet him. But there's another reason for grooming, and that's to help to keep your Cavalier healthy. Grooming frees the coat of dirt and grime and helps spread skin oils evenly throughout the coat. As you groom, you may find and eliminate small problems that can grow to be big problems, such as fleas, ticks, or any unusual skin growths.

In addition to keeping your dog clean, a grooming session can help you bond with your dog. It offers one-on-one time, with no distractions. If you have multiple dogs, this is each dog's time to be alone with you. Cavaliers love being near their person, so your dog will love this special time set aside for just the two of you.

Grooming for Good Health

Regular grooming sessions do more than keep your dog looking good. A grooming session is also the perfect time to go over your dog for health reasons. Run your hands over your dog during grooming. If he has any lumps or bumps, you'll feel them, or if he pulls away or cringes at your touch, he may have a bruise or sore that bears watching.

Grooming will allow you to feel a tick if one has latched onto your dog. Also, brushing and combing may disturb fleas, or you may notice dark flecks of flea dirt.

As you cut or grind your Cavalier's nails, check the pads of his feet for cuts or scrapes, and feel between the toes for any growths. Those long, lovely Cavalier ears can hide an infection, so make sure that an ear check is a part of your grooming routine. The ear should be pink, with no

discharge and no odour. Check your dog's teeth, too. If you notice a buildup of plaque, it may be time for a professional teeth cleaning.

Grooming Supplies

You'll need a few items on hand to properly groom your Cavalier:

Soft, small slicker brush. A slicker brush has wire bristles set at an angle. Use this tool on the ears.

Greyhound comb or a couple of combs with teeth of various widths. Use this to straighten hair and to gently pick apart mats.

Flea comb. A flea comb is a very fine-toothed comb that can trap fleas as you comb.

Small pin brush. A pin brush has widespread bristles, each of which is

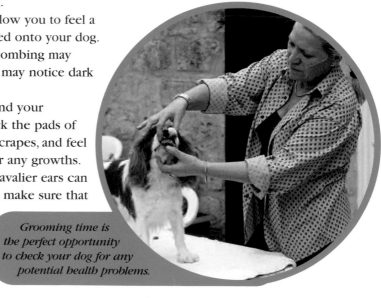

Grooming time is the perfect opportunity to check your dog for any potential health problems.

Grooming Table

You may want to invest in a grooming table. Grooming tables are dog-sized folding tables that have a nonskid surface and put your dog at your height for grooming. Raising your dog off the floor can really save your back, and many dogs are calmer on a table and less likely to try to get away. You can add a grooming arm, which is shaped like an inverted "L" and extends over the table. Attach a grooming loop to the arm, then slip the loop over your dog's head to help to keep his head up and out of your way as you groom.

If you don't want to buy a grooming table, put a nonskid mat on top of a clothes dryer or on any table. I've found that my bed works well. It's relatively high, and I just cover a corner with a sheet. The dogs seem more willing to lie down on the softer surface, and I can brush my older dog while he's stretched out on his side.

No matter what you choose for a grooming surface, never leave your dog unattended. If you're using a grooming loop, he could hang himself, and if your dog is loose on a high surface, he could jump off and injure himself.

topped with a tiny round ball so that each bristle looks a bit like a straight pin. Use this brush on the body and to gently remove any tangles in the "feathering" on the tail and legs.

Boar-bristle brush or any soft-bristled brush for finishing. It will smooth your Cavalier's coat and add a bit of sheen.

Small scissors. Use the scissors for trimming hair between the footpads. You may want to trim this hair to help with traction and to eliminate mud buildup in the winter. Trimming in the summer will reduce the amount of dirt your dog brings in.

Ear cleaner. Your veterinarian may sell this, or you can buy it at a pet shop.

Nail clippers and/or a grinding tool. There are two main types of nail clippers on the market. One is the guillotine type, in which a blade slides across and cuts the nail. The other looks more like a heavy-duty pair of scissors. Choose the kind you are most comfortable using. There is also a clipper on the market that senses the location of the quick, which is the vein in each nail. A light flashes green when it's safe to cut. If your dog has dark nails, this clipper is worth the money.

Brushing

Brushing helps to prevent mats—large snarls of hair that, if not combed out, can get bigger and tighter, eventually pulling and tearing the skin.

A Cavalier's coat is soft and silky, and mats can build up behind the elbows and especially on the ears. Mats hold dirt and make a great place for fleas to hide.

Your Cavalier may need a quick combing and brushing every day, or you may only need to groom two or three times a week.

How to Brush Your Cavalier

Check first to see if any mats are present that need detangling. If you find a mat, dust it with cornstarch, and gently work it apart using a wide-toothed comb or your fingers. Now, lightly dampen the coat before brushing. You can use plain water, or you may want to add a bit of coat conditioner to the water to help prevent tangles. Start with those lovely long ears. Gently brush the length of the ear with a small slicker brush. Make sure that you don't brush so hard that you hurt those sensitive ears. Use the slicker brush on the longer hair on the back of the legs as well.

For the rest of the body, either use the slicker or a pin brush. Start just behind the

head, and brush in the direction that the hair grows. You want to get through all the coat, but don't brush so vigorously that you hurt your dog. A slicker brush, especially, can scratch your dog's skin if too much pressure is applied.

Comb your dog after brushing to further straighten the hair. If you suspect fleas, use a flea comb to trap any of those nasty critters. Finally, go over your dog with the soft-bristle brush. This will give the coat a smooth, shiny look.

Bathing

If you plan to show your Cavalier, a bath will be on the agenda every week.

Regular brushing prevents mats, especially on the Cavalier's ears.

If your Cavalier is a homebody, you might be able to bathe less frequently. If you're brushing and combing every day, you might be able to bathe just once a month. Many people with Cavaliers enjoy cuddling with them or letting them sleep on the bed, and if that's the case for you, you'll want a clean dog sharing your sheets.

Before popping your Cavalier into the suds, brush out the coat and remove mats or tangles because these only get worse when they're wet. Next, get everything ready for the bath *before* you retrieve your dog. Your kitchen sink might be just the right size for your Cavalier, and it will be easier on your back than bending over the bath. Wherever you bathe your dog, make sure that there's a rubber mat on the bottom of the bath to prevent him from slipping. Gather up plenty of towels, and get the dog shampoo. Always use a dog shampoo. (Human shampoo is not at the correct pH for a dog.)

Many people put cotton balls in their dog's ears to keep water out. My experience is that the dog will just keep shaking his head until the cotton comes out. I shampoo from the head back and do the ears and head separately, taking each ear in turn and using very little soap and hand rinsing, keeping my hand between the opening of the ear and the ear flap. For the face and muzzle, I wipe with a damp cloth and don't use soap at all. You also can add a drop or two of

SENIOR DOG TIP

Grooming the Older Dog

Older dogs need grooming just as much as young dogs, but you'll need to be a bit more careful. An older dog may have developed odd lumps or bumps, such as benign fatty tumours, so avoid raking over them with your brush. An older dog also may have arthritis, which can make standing for a long grooming session painful. A vigorous brushing may be too much for your senior.

Break up senior grooming sessions. Do the nails one day, then brush his coat another, and do his ears on yet another day.

mineral oil or artificial tears to both eyes and ears to help to prevent soap from getting in.

Pet shops sell wonderful gadgets that attach to your showerhead or to your tap and act as a dog shower. Otherwise, get a saucepan or a large unbreakable jug to use for getting your dog wet.

How to Bathe Your Cavalier

First, adjust the water temperature before you put your dog in the bath. That way, you won't risk burning sensitive toes, and you can use both hands to hold your dog instead of using one to hold the dog and the other to adjust the water.

Next, go and get your dog. Most dogs aren't fond of baths, so don't call him—go and get him. Close the bathroom door if you're in the bathroom. If your dog gets away from you, he won't spread soap and water all over the house.

Put your dog in the bath and wet him all over, either with the spray head of your

You may want to consider investing in a grooming table, a dog-sized folding table with a nonskid surface.

doggy shower attachment, or with a pan or jug. Make sure that he is wet to the skin. Work shampoo into his coat. Don't forget his stomach, feet, and tail. Rinse. Repeat. Rinse again, making sure that all the soap is rinsed out. Soap residue can make your dog itch. About ½ cup (118.3 ml) of vinegar added to the rinse water helps to get rid of the soap. If you want, you also can add a coat conditioner to the final rinse.

Lift your dog from the bath. Don't let him jump out because he could hurt himself. He'll want to shake, and you'll be amazed at how much water will come off such a small dog. Blot with towels to get rid of as much water as you can. A Cavalier can air dry, or you can use a hair dryer. If you use a human hair dryer, use one with an air-only setting; otherwise, human dryers are too hot for dogs and can burn their skin. Use your pin brush to brush hair up and against the grain, training the dryer at the base of the hair. Keep the dryer nozzle moving so that no one spot on your dog gets too hot.

After a bath is a good time to cut nails because the water will have softened them a bit.

Nail Care

Long nails can make it hard for a dog to walk, and really long nails can curl around and puncture the paw pads. Nails grow at different rates, and if you walk your dog regularly on rough concrete pavements, you may never need to cut them. If your dog spends most of his time in the garden or in the house, though, you'll need to trim nails once a week or once every two weeks.

If you're not comfortable with nail clippers, consider a grinding wheel. This is a high-speed drum that grinds the nail away. Many dogs who resist having their nails cut don't seem to mind a grinder. If you just can't do it yourself, make a regular trip to your local groomer and have her cut your dog's nails.

How to Trim Your Cavalier's Nails

Nail care is important, so get your dog used to having his feet handled when he's a puppy. Hold a foot and play with the toes, then give him a treat.

If you're using nail clippers, cut the tip of the nail off, right where the nail starts to curve. If your dog has white nails, you'll be able to see the quick,

Sticky Stuff

If your dog gets something sticky in his coat, here are some tips for getting it out. (Only use scissors as a last resort because you don't want a big hole in your dog's fur, and you could accidentally hurt him with this sharp tool.) Most types of food, like candyfloss, lollipop residue, and ice cream will wash out with warm water and a bit of dog shampoo. An exception is chewing gum. If your dog gets gum tangled in his coat, rub the gum with some peanut butter or vegetable oil and then gently work it out with your fingers. You also can try freezing the gum between a couple of ice cubes. If you use ice, be sure that you don't hold the ice directly on your dog's skin. These techniques also work with tar or tree sap, and they're safe because they aren't filled with chemicals that could harm your dog.

the blood vessel that runs through the middle of the nail. If your dog's nails are black, you'll have to guess. Try not to hit the quick. If you do, your dog's nail will bleed. Use a bit of styptic powder to stop the bleeding, or if you don't have any, cornflour will work.

If you decide to use a grinder, start slowly. Turn on the grinder and let the dog get used to the noise. Hold the body of the grinder against his foot so that he can feel the vibrations. Start with one foot. Grind the nails, then stop and give your dog a treat. If he's still relatively calm, do another foot. If he's struggling, stop with just one foot. Do another foot the next day, and so on. Eventually, your dog will allow you to do all his feet.

Ear Care

Ear care is an important part of grooming a Cavalier. Dogs with long ears that cover the ear opening are prone to infections because that beautiful long earflap keeps air from circulating. The ear stays dark and moist, and that's the perfect climate for a yeast infection.

How to Care for Your Cavalier's Ears

Outside, keep the fur mat-free with frequent brushing and combing. Inside, make an inspection a weekly habit. Clean out the ear with a cotton ball or soft cloth soaked in ear cleanser. The inside of your dog's ear should be light pink. There

should be no discharge and no odour. If your dog is scratching and digging at his ear, tilting his head sideways, or if the ear is red, inflamed, or has a smelly discharge, take your dog to the veterinarian for treatment.

Eye Care

Your Cavalier's lovely brown eyes give him that melting, soft expression that makes it so hard to resist when he wants a treat.

How to Care for Your Cavalier's Eyes

There's not much you can do for your dog's eyes except to look closely at them once a week or so. They should be clear, and he should not be blinking excessively or rubbing at them with his paw. There shouldn't be any discharge or swelling.

Introduce your Cavalier to nail trimming slowly so that you can desensitise him to the process.

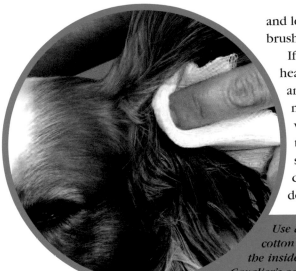

and let dry, then brush off. Always brush *away* from your dog's eyes.

If the stain is constant and very heavy, try cleaning the stained area and then applying a thin layer of nappy rash ointment. Dust lightly with a medicated powder. The tears should roll off instead of soaking in and staining. Again, be careful not to get anything in your dog's eyes.

Use a soft cloth or cotton ball to clean the inside flap of your Cavalier's ears.

Sometimes seeds or dirt can get in your dog's eye and irritate it. If you can see a bit of dirt, try applying a few drops of artificial tears to see if they will rinse out the problem. Otherwise, if you notice a problem, take a trip to the veterinarian.

How to Remove Tear Stains

Some dogs have tear stains on their faces. These stains are not a health concern, but they can be unsightly. You can remove these or at least lessen the stain, but be very careful not to get any of the cleaning agents into your dog's eyes.

Boric acid or boric ointment can remove the stain. Soak a cotton ball in boric acid and gently wipe the stain, or use a dab of boric acid ointment on the stain. Another technique is to make a thin paste of cornflour and hydrogen peroxide. Apply the paste to the stain

Dental Care

Dogs don't usually get cavities the way people do, but keeping your Cavalier's teeth clean should be a part of your routine. Plaque can build up on a dog's teeth, and it eventually will harden into tartar that continues to build up on tooth surfaces. That tartar causes gum abscesses, and bacteria from those abscesses can circulate through your dog's blood system and cause pneumonia, or heart, liver, or kidney problems.

How to Care for Your Cavalier's Teeth

Guard your Cavalier's health by brushing his teeth regularly. Start when your dog is a puppy. If you can do it every day, great, but even two or three times a week is helpful, and once a week is better than nothing.

Start by wrapping your finger in gauze and rubbing your finger over

Looking Good

Your Child and Grooming

An older child can definitely groom a Cavalier, with the possible exception of ear cleaning, nail trimming, and cutting foot fur. Show the child how to gently comb or brush with the grain of the fur. If she will be using the slicker brush on ears and legs, make sure that she understands that she must be gentle. Don't let a child pull or tug at hair. If the dog shows signs of discomfort, the child should stop grooming.

Very young children may not be able to really groom the dog, but they can be taught to brush gently with a soft bristle brush. Always supervise small children and emphasise the need to be gentle. Stop the grooming at once if the dog looks like the grooming is hurting him.

your dog's teeth and gums. Use a dab of flavoured doggy toothpaste. These come in meaty flavours that your dog will enjoy. Never use toothpaste made for humans; they are too foamy, and the added fluoride is not good for your dog.

Once your dog accepts your gauze-wrapped finger, advance to a toothbrush. Choose pretreated tooth wipes, a small plastic brush that fits over your finger, or a special toothbrush that looks much like your own.

As you clean your dog's teeth, take note of any problems that may need

Guard your Cavalier's health by regularly inspecting his mouth and brushing his teeth.

attention. If your dog's breath is bad or smells different from normal, he may have a problem with his teeth. If he is drooling, pawing at his mouth, having trouble eating hard kibble, or doesn't want to play with his toys or chew on a bone, it may be time for a veterinary visit.

Even if you brush your dog's teeth regularly, your veterinarian may recommend a professional cleaning. That's not surprising, because humans brush and floss, and still rely on the dentist to do a more thorough cleaning. During a professional cleaning, your veterinarian will anaesthetise your dog, remove any tartar buildup, and then clean and polish your dog's teeth. If your Cavalier has any broken or cracked teeth, the vet will pull them at this time. She may run a blood test before the cleaning, especially if your dog is older. This is a safety precaution to make sure that your dog won't have any problems with the anaesthesia.

Cavalier Accessories

Many toy dogs wear bows in their hair or get their nails painted. You could do your dog's nails, but with all that foot fur, no one would see it, and Cavaliers

The Expert Knows

Collar and Harness Care

Your dog's collar or harness can get dirty from both natural oils from his coat and from external dirt and grime, so give it a scrub. Leather collars and harnesses can be cleaned with saddle soap. If your collar or harness is nylon, use an old toothbrush and a bit of shampoo to scrub out the dirt. Make sure that you rinse thoroughly, or leftover soap may make your dog itch.

generally don't wear bows, but it's up to you. The same goes for rhinestone-studded collars.

In very cold weather, your Cavalier may be happy to have a sweater, especially if he's a senior. Most of the time, though, he is happy to wear just his own striking fur coat.

Grooming involves more than just keeping your Cavalier looking good. It helps to keep him healthy by removing dirt (and maybe fleas) from his coat, and as you groom, you also can look for any cuts, scrapes, or unusual lumps and bumps. In addition, grooming is a great way to spend time with your dog!

Chapter 5

Feeling Good

You may not be able to protect your Cavalier from everything, but you can guard against the deadliest diseases and keep your dog as healthy as possible with good food, exercise, and regular checkups with your veterinarian. This chapter will help you find a veterinarian, learn about breed-specific and general illnesses that could affect your Cavalier, deal with emergencies, and explore alternative therapies.

Finding a Veterinarian

Finding a veterinarian whom you like and trust is important. Your Cavalier needs annual checkups to keep him healthy—including vaccinations—and if there's an emergency, you'll want to know that help is available. If you don't already have a family vet, talk to your Cavalier's breeder and to friends who have dogs.

Consider Distance

Consider distance when you're making your choice. Your breeder may recommend a wonderful practice, but it may take you 45 minutes to drive there. You may not mind the drive for a wellness checkup, but if an emergency coincides with a bad weather, that veterinarian may not be practical.

Call Local Practices

Call the practices in your area and ask how they handle emergencies. Some practices share after-hours calls with other area veterinarians. Some have an answering service and will contact your vet and have her return your call.

Think about how many vets are in the practice.

With a smaller practice, you'll see the same veterinarian every time and she'll get to know both you and your dog. The disadvantage is that if you need to go to another practice in an emergency, that veterinarian won't know your dog's history or have access to his records. In a multi-veterinarian

Keep your dog healthy with annual veterinary visits.

practice, you may not always see the same vet each time, but all of the veterinarians will have access to your dog's complete medical history when they need it.

Visit Veterinarian Practices

If possible, visit veterinarian practices. Waiting rooms should be clean, and the staff should be friendly. During your dog's first visit, pay attention to how the veterinarian handles your dog and how she responds to your questions. No matter how highly a practice is recommended, if you're uncomfortable for any reason, or your questions and concerns are not answered to your satisfaction, find another veterinarian. Your dog's health care is a partnership between you and the vet. You need to be comfortable with your choice.

Visiting the Vet

Visiting the vet will probably never be your dog's favourite activity, but it doesn't have to be traumatic. Take a pocketful of treats and have everyone give your puppy one, from the receptionist who checks you in to the vet tech who may take your dog's temperature to the veterinarian. Have an upbeat attitude, and your Cavalier will learn from you and take the visit in stride.

Puppy's First Vet Visit

Once you've chosen a veterinarian, schedule an appointment for your

FAMILY-FRIENDLY TIP

How to Prepare Your Child for a Vet Visit

Consider your child's age before you allow her to go with you to the vet's. Young children may become upset if they think that someone is hurting their dog, and this will, in turn, upset the dog. In addition, very young children may not understand that they should leave other dogs in the waiting room alone. You'll have enough on your hands managing your dog without having to worry about your child as well.

Generally, children less than seven years of age should stay out of the exam room. If you have an older child, explain ahead of time what will happen during the exam. Tell the child that your dog will be getting shots to keep him well. The doctor will be looking at your dog's ears, eyes, and mouth. She'll be listening to the heart and lungs, and she will take his temperature. Explain to the child that she must remain calm and quiet to help the dog remain calm and quiet.

puppy as soon after he comes home as possible. Your veterinarian will give him a thorough checkup, and if it's

time for vaccinations, she'll give those. This is a good time to go over any questions you might have concerning diet or grooming. Ask for a demonstration of nail clipping and brushing teeth, and ask the veterinarian to show you how to properly clean your Cavalier's ears.

This visit will be the first of your annual visits that will keep your Cavalier healthy.

The Annual Vet Visit

Each year, your dog will get whatever vaccinations you and your vet have decided on. Your vet will check your dog's teeth and may recommend a professional cleaning. She'll listen to your dog's heart, and will catch any abnormalities early. As your Cavalier gets older, the annual visit may include blood work.

Neutering

Unless you're seriously considering breeding or showing your dog, have him or her neutered. (Male dogs are castrated, and female dogs are spayed.)

For females, in addition to the benefit of no unwanted litters, spaying before the third heat lowers the chance of mammary tumours. Spaying also ends the risk of pyometra and other reproductive infections, as well as eliminates the twice-yearly "season."

For males, neutering lessens the chance that they will stray from home in search of a female. Neutering also prevents prostate problems and may help to curb aggression toward other males. Intact males are more likely to mark their territory inside the house, even if they are housetrained, and this can be a very hard habit to break.

Neither spaying nor castrating is particularly complicated, and with a healthy young dog there shouldn't be any problems. Castrating is the easier of the two surgeries because the testicles are external, but even with spaying, your dog should be home the next day. Keep an eye on the incision. Redness or puffiness could indicate infection.

Vaccinations

What type of vaccinations your dog gets and when are topics to discuss with your veterinarian. More and more, veterinarians are vaccinating for deadly diseases only and letting other vaccinations be optional, depending on the dog and where you live.

Vaccination Schedules

Initially, puppies are vaccinated at 8 weeks, then 12 weeks, then 16 weeks, and then annually. Some veterinarians also may recommend shots at 18 to 20 weeks and then annually. Get a health record with your puppy so that you'll

Pet Health Insurance

Pet health insurance is available but benefits vary, so enrol in a plan that will meet your needs. Some policies cover basic veterinary visits for things like vaccinations, but most policies exclude vaccinations and neutering. Basic insurance also may have a cap for illnesses such as cancer, and many policies won't cover advanced medical techniques. If they do, they may require a special rider to the basic policy. Most insurance policies won't cover pre-existing conditions, and some won't cover illnesses if a breed is predisposed to them. For example, a policy might not cover mitral valve disease in your Cavalier, even if you bought the policy long before your dog ever developed the problem.

know what, if any, shots have been given by the breeder.

Dogs used to be vaccinated every year with every vaccine, but the trend now is to vaccinate as needed. Dogs who travel a lot or who participate in dog shows may need more shots than the stay-at-home pet or the older dog. Drug companies are working on vaccines that will give protection for three to four years. For example, distemper vaccines are now on the market that protect for at least three years.

Core Vaccines

Core vaccines are those vaccines that veterinarians feel that your dog must have. These have changed recently. In my area, veterinarians no longer include leptospirosis in the core, but they vaccinate against distemper and parvovirus because they can be fatal. Rabies is not present in the UK, but if you are travelling abroad your dog will need to be vaccinated.

Negative Reactions to Vaccines

Sometimes a dog can have a negative reaction to a vaccine. After your Cavalier has been vaccinated, stay at the veterinarian's surgery for a while to see if he has a reaction, like face swelling or breathing difficulties. If he does, the staff will be available to counteract it.

If you already know that your dog reacts to vaccinations, tell your vet before she gives the shots. To help to prevent a bad reaction, she may break up the shots instead of giving them in a combination. She also might give one shot at one appointment and the other vaccines on a separate occasion. She's not doing this to inconvenience you or to make more money—she's doing it to protect your dog.

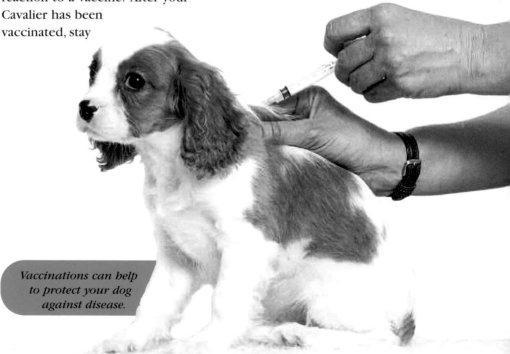

Vaccinations can help to protect your dog against disease.

SENIOR DOG TIP

Coping With a Senior's Declining Health

Your dog can enjoy his senior years in spite of failing senses, but he'll need help from you to do it—like a baby aspirin to help to ease aching joints, an elevated bed, or a special mattress. You may need to build a ramp from the porch to the ground if climbing stairs is a problem, and if he's allowed on the furniture, make sure that someone is there to lift him on and off the sofa.

Dogs can manage quite well with diminished sight and hearing, but you'll need to help. Teach your deaf dog to respond to hand signals, or stamp on the floor to get his attention. If your Cavalier's eyesight is dimming, this is not the time to rearrange the furniture. In addition, your dog may need to make more trips outdoors to relieve himself. Be attentive to his needs. A dog who managed quite nicely going out three or four times a day may need to go out six or seven, including in the middle of the night. Your veterinarian may prescribe a special food for your dog, or there may be daily medications.

Be patient with your senior. He's been your constant companion, providing lots of kisses and snuggles. It's time to pay him back by keeping him as happy and comfortable as possible.

Common Vaccinations

Dogs are commonly vaccinated against the following diseases.

Bordetella

Bordetella, or kennel cough, is a highly contagious airborne disease that produces a dry, hacking cough. It can be treated with antibiotics and is rarely serious, but because it is so contagious, most boarding kennels require the bordetella vaccination. The vaccine doesn't cover all the varieties of kennel cough, but it can help.

Coronavirus

Coronavirus is a highly contagious virus that causes diarrhoea for about a week. The diarrhoea may be somewhat orange in colour, and it will have a strong odour. The dog may need to be treated for dehydration. This disease is rarely fatal, and some Cavaliers have a

Roundworms commonly pass from mother dogs to their puppies.

Distemper

Distemper is frequently fatal. This virus is extremely contagious and is most dangerous in puppies three to six months old and in dogs more than six years of age. Symptoms include vomiting, coughing, and fever, and the dog usually dies.

Parvovirus

Parvovirus is another deadly disease. Puppies are very susceptible and generally don't survive, especially if they are vomiting and have bloody diarrhoea. The dog may have a fever, and he will be lethargic and depressed. Dogs with mild cases usually recover, but again, puppies tend to lose the battle.

Hepatitis

Hepatitis is spread through the faeces and urine of infected animals. A dog with a moderate case will have a fever and be lethargic. He may be reluctant to move and have abdominal tenderness and pale mucous membranes.

reaction to the vaccine, so you might decide against it. Discuss your concerns with your veterinarian.

He generally will recover within one to five days, but in a severe case, he may vomit, have diarrhoea, and develop a cough. Sudden death may result.

Leptospirosis

Leptospirosis is a bacteria transmitted through urine, especially that of rats and mice. Symptoms include vomiting, fever, and a reluctance to move. Renal failure may occur. Severe cases can be fatal, but unless you are in an area where your dog will be exposed to the urine of rats and mice, you may decide to skip this shot. The leptospirosis vaccine can cause reactions in Cavaliers.

Lyme Disease

The deer tick spreads Lyme disease, and the disease produces lethargy, loss of appetite, and lameness. It can be treated with antibiotics. Where you live

and what you do with your dog will determine whether or not your veterinarian recommends this vaccination.

Rabies

Rabies is a virus that attacks the central nervous system in mammals. It is spread by the saliva of an infected animal, such as bats or foxes. Once symptoms appear, there is no cure. Symptoms include nervousness, anxiety, and sensitivity to light and sound. A dog may become vicious or have trouble breathing, as though something were stuck in his throat. Rabies is not present in the UK, but can be prevented with a vaccination if you are travelling overseas.

Parasites

Canine parasites may be either internal

or external. Internal parasites are generally some type of worm that lives inside the dog, using resources that the dog needs for himself. External parasites also feed on the dog, but they are on the outside, piercing the skin to reach their food supply—your dog's blood.

Internal Parasites

Common internal parasites include heartworms, hookworms, roundworms, tapeworms, and whipworms.

Heartworms

Heartworm is spread by mosquitoes and has been found on every continent except Antarctica. The heartworm lives in a dog's heart,

eventually totally clogging it and making it impossible for the heart to effectively pump blood.

Heartworm is not found in the UK, but is present in parts of Europe. If you are travelling abroad with your dog discuss a preventive with your vet.

Hookworms

Hookworm eggs are passed in the faeces and can live in the soil. They also can be passed from a mother to her puppies. Hookworms cause anaemia.

Roundworms

Roundworms, like hookworms, can contaminate the soil, and the eggs can live in the soil for years. Most puppies are born with these worms. The larvae live in the mother but don't infect her. The roundworm can cause diarrhoea, abdominal pain, and dehydration. In puppies, they can cause intestinal blockages or perforation of the intestine.

Tapeworms

Tapeworms are relatively harmless, and there are rarely any signs that they are present, other than

Check your Cavalier for fleas and ticks after he's been playing outside.

fragments in the stool that look like grains of rice. Fleas spread tapeworms.

Whipworms

Whipworms can cause inflammation of the colon, and your dog may experience abdominal pain, weight loss, dehydration, and in severe cases, anaemia. If your Cavalier has bloody diarrhoea, he may have whipworms. Whipworms contaminate the soil, and there's no way to get rid of them short of paving your entire garden.

External Parasites

Common external parasites include fleas and ticks.

Fleas

Fleas are nasty parasites that spread disease. They can give your dog tapeworms and cause itching. One flea

Darcy's Battle With MVD

Darcy, a sweet tri-colour Cavalier, was just three years old when she was diagnosed with mitral valve disease. Each year, she received annual X-rays, electrocardiograms, and echocardiograms to monitor the problem, and in November of 2005, tests showed that the disease was progressing. Seven different medicines helped to keep her going for several months, but finally, the disease won.

In June of 2006, Darcy lost her battle with heart disease. In September of that year, Darcy's owners, Kim and Jerry Thornton of Lake Forest, California, started the Darcy Fund to finance research into the causes and cure of chronic valvular disease, also known as mitral valve disease, the most common form of heart disease affecting dogs. The fund has been set up in conjunction with the American Cavalier King Charles Spaniel Club's Charitable Trust, an organisation formed in 2002 for the protection of the health of the Cavalier King Charles Spaniel. While the Darcy Fund is linked to Cavaliers, any discoveries it helps to fund have the potential to benefit all dogs. For more information, visit http://ackcsccharitabletrust.org/.

can bite your dog up to 400 times!

The easiest way to check for fleas is to roll your dog over and inspect the area toward the hind legs, where the hair is thinner. You may see fleas, or you may find "flea dirt," dark flecks of flea faeces that turn red when placed on a dampened paper towel.

Use a flea comb to help to eliminate fleas. If your dog is truly infested, give him a bath. Don't forget to wash his bed regularly as well because that's where the flea eggs will be. Then, consult your vet on the best course of action to take, and talk to her about a monthly flea preventive as well.

Ticks

Ticks are external parasites that can spread disease to both you and your dog. In fact, they may give your dog Lyme disease, or tick paralysis.

Make a habit of running your hands over your dog once or twice a week, maybe when you're grooming him. If you feel a bump, it may be a well-fed tick. If you find a tick on your dog, use tweezers to remove it. Grasp the tick firmly near where it is attached to your dog. Pull gently and slowly. Don't crush, jerk, or squeeze the tick—and do not handle the tick in any way. (If you do, wash your hands immediately.) Wash the area on your dog where the tick was imbedded, and disinfect.

Never use any kind of flame to remove the tick. Fire will get the tick's attention all right, but you run the risk of burning your dog. If you can't remove the tick yourself, take your dog to the vet immediately.

Many flea preventives also discourage ticks. If ticks are a problem in your area, talk to your vet about a flea preventive that also fights ticks.

Breed-Specific Illnesses

No breed of dog or mixed breed, for that matter, is perfect. Any dog can become ill, and many dogs have specific health problems. Your Cavalier can be a happy, healthy dog, but there are some breed-specific health problems of which you should be aware.

Brachycephalic Airway Obstruction Syndrome (BAOS)

Brachycephalic airway obstruction syndrome is an inherited condition that can be life-threatening. Although the Cavalier doesn't have as flat a face as the King Charles Spaniel or the Pug, it is short enough to cause problems with breathing. The shortened muzzle means that the Cavalier may have an elongated soft palate, stenotic nares (narrow nostrils), and problems with the larynx.

Symptoms

If your Cavalier breathes through his mouth, snores excessively, gags, has a pale or bluish tongue and gums, or

Ticks are external parasites that often lurk in grassy and wooded areas.

can't exercise moderately without tiring quickly and breathing heavily, BAOS may be the problem.

Treatment

If symptoms are mild, don't let your Cavalier get overheated, especially in the summer. Keep his weight down, because obesity can add to the problem. If the problem is severe, surgery may be necessary to reduce the elongated palate and to open the nasal passages.

Dogs can be allergic to the same things that cause a reaction in people, such as food.

Hip Dysplasia

Typically, hip dysplasia is thought of as a problem in large-breed dogs, but any dog of any size can have hip dysplasia. In a dysplastic hip, the socket of the hip joint is malformed and wears on the head of the femur, which does not fit properly into the joint. Sometimes, the femur comes out of the joint altogether, causing pain and damage to ligaments.

Symptoms

Dogs with hip dysplasia may limp after exercise or may have trouble going up and down stairs. A dog also may develop arthritis in the joint.

Treatment

Mild cases can be treated with exercise and diet; severe cases need corrective surgery.

Mitral Valve Disease (MVD)

Mitral valve disease affects 50 to 60 percent of all Cavaliers. This is a progressive, degenerative disease of the heart valves, mainly the mitral valve on the left side of the heart.

Symptoms

The first indication of

Ear infections are common in dogs with soft floppy ears.

exception. Patellar luxation occurs when the kneecap, or patella, shifts out of position.

Symptoms

A Cavalier with a luxating patella may stand with his toes turned in and may throw his weight forward onto his front legs. He also may limp or hold the leg so that it barely touches the ground. If you notice your Cavalier favouring a hind leg, and there's no evidence of an injury, it may be the patella.

Treatment

The kneecap may pop back into its groove by itself, or a veterinarian may need to do it. A dog will be lame while the kneecap is out of place.

Syringomyelia

Syringomyelia is sometimes called "neck scratchers' disease" because a sign is that the dog scratches the air near his neck. With this disease, obstruction of the flow of cerebrospinal fluid causes pressure that pushes the cerebellum out the back of the skull, which in turn causes pressure on the spine.

Symptoms

Dogs with syringomyelia may scratch constantly at their head, shoulders, or

this disease is a heart murmur. As the disease progresses, the dog may cough because the enlarged heart is pressing on the airways. The dog will tire easily. Some dogs will retain fluid in the abdomen. Gums may be pale, and the pulse weak.

Because the disease progresses at different rates, a Cavalier may show no indications of the disease, other than a heart murmur.

Treatment

Some dogs can manage for years on a variety of medications. At present, there is no genetic marker for this disease.

Patellar Luxation

Many toy dogs have a tendency toward patellar luxation, and the Cavalier is no ears, often on one side only. They may yelp or whine, and they may suffer a lack of coordination. A dog may collapse or suddenly fall over. Symptoms usually appear between the ages of six months to three years.

Treatment

Magnetic resonance imaging (MRI) will detect syringomyelia, but the disease is progressive and incurable. Depending on how rapidly the disease progresses, medicine may relieve symptoms and allow the dog to enjoy life.

General Illnesses

Some health issues, such as allergies, cancer, and ear infections, can apply to any breed.

Allergies

Dogs can be allergic to the same things that cause a reaction in people, such as pollen, dander, and foods.

Symptoms

With dogs, although eyes and nose may run, allergies frequently mean itchy skin. If your dog is allergic to his food, he may lick and chew his feet or the base of his tail. If your Cavalier is scratching and it appears to be seasonal, there may be a problem

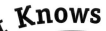

The Expert Knows

What Is a Holistic Veterinarian?

Using the term broadly, a holistic veterinarian treats the whole dog. That is, rather than diagnosing a problem based on symptoms alone, the veterinarian will go further, considering all aspects of the dog—his general health, his age, his temperament, and his overall lifestyle—to see if changes in any of these areas might affect the choice of treatment. Holistic veterinarians are more likely to consider alternatives to Western medicine, and they may use acupuncture, herbal treatments, and homeopathy.

with pollen.

Treatment

Talk to your vet about ways to ease the symptoms. She may suggest a special diet if the allergy is food related, or she will advise you on ways to soothe your dog's itchy skin.

Cancer

Cancer is a disease in which cells run amok. Cancer cells grow abnormally and rapidly, destroying good cells in the process. Cancer can take many forms and may attack the skin, blood, or organs.

Symptoms

If you discover a rapidly growing growth on your dog, or if you notice swollen lymph nodes, get your dog to your veterinarian immediately. Other signs of cancer may include a sore that doesn't heal, difficulty breathing, lack of appetite, lethargy, blood in the urine or faeces, or lameness or stiffness that doesn't go away.

Treatment

Many cancers can be cured if caught early enough, and progress is being made in treating all types. Surgery, chemotherapy, and radiation therapy are all tools that, if they can't cure your dog, can at least put the disease in remission or buy him a bit more time.

Ear Infections

Yeast infections are a common problem in dogs with soft floppy ears like the Cavalier.

Symptoms

If your Cavalier is digging and scratching at his ears, rubbing his head on the ground, or holding his head at an angle, take a look inside his ears. If they are red or appear

The right amount of exercise is key to your Cavalier's health.

inflamed, it's time for a trip to the vet.

Treatment
Depending on the severity of the problem, your vet may give you a topical treatment or an oral drug, or both.

First Aid
No matter what the medical emergency, the first thing to remember is to remain calm. It's easy to panic if your dog gets hurt or appears ill, but by staying calm, you can act appropriately, and your manner will help to calm your dog. If any problem, such as vomiting or diarrhoea, gets worse over

several hours or continues past 24 hours, call your vet.

Learn First-Aid Techniques
Many first-aid techniques for humans apply to dogs as well, such as applying a pressure bandage to a bleeding wound. Consider a taking a first-aid course for animals. Check with your vet about first aid classes in your area.

Make a First-Aid Kit
Put together a basic first-aid kit. Again, this is similar to a kit for humans. It should include gauze pads, a roll of gauze, hydrogen peroxide, an antibiotic ointment, scissors, thermometer, baby aspirin, tweezers, and artificial tears. Benadryl is also a good addition in case your dog has an allergic reaction to a bee sting or a bug bite. Include your veterinarian's phone number in the kit as well.

Monitor Vital Signs
A dog's normal temperature is between 100° and 102°F (37.8° and 38.9°C). Learn to take your dog's temperature. If the temperature goes below 100°F (37.8°C) or above 104°F (40°C), call your veterinarian.

Learn to take your dog's pulse

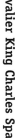

Your Doggy First-Aid Kit

Here are some basic items you should have in case of emergencies. If you travel frequently with your dog, keep a basic kit in your car.

- antibiotic ointment
- artificial tears
- baby aspirin
- benadryl
- Betadine
- gauze pads
- hydrogen peroxide

- roll of gauze
- scissors
- telephone number of your veterinarian
- thermometer
- tweezers

and make a note of his normal pulse rate when at rest. A dog's pulse rate is between 80 and 140. The smaller your Cavalier, the higher the number will be.

How to Deal With an Emergency

If your dog is severely injured, you may need to muzzle him. When hurt, even the most loving dog may snap or bite. Because Cavaliers have a very small muzzle, this may not be practical, especially because you don't want to restrict his breathing in any way. Another solution is to wrap your dog in a blanket with the ends extending out past his head. You also could use a magazine. This will keep him from turning his head and help to keep his muzzle away from your hands while you try to help him.

If you suspect spinal injuries, transport your dog on a blanket or board. Try to move him as little as possible.

If you suspect that your dog has ingested something poisonous, contact your veterinarian immediately.

If you need to get your dog to the veterinarian, call first. This gives the staff time to prepare for the emergency before your dog arrives.

Alternative Therapies

Your veterinarian may use medical techniques that are not part of Western veterinary care. In fact, many veterinarians use alternative therapies to complement Western teaching, giving their patients the best of both worlds.

Acupuncture

Acupuncture has been used on humans for more than 4,500 years and on animals for about 2,000 years. An acupuncturist uses very thin needles to stimulate acupoints to help with healing. Acupoints contain concentrated levels of nerve endings, lymphatics, and blood vessels, and these points occur on meridians or energy paths. Acupuncture can increase blood flow, lower heart rate, and improve immune function. It also releases endorphins, the body's natural painkillers, and smaller amounts of cortisol, an anti-inflammatory steroid.

Chiropractic

Chiropractic treatment realigns bones that may be out of position as a result of a fall or bumping into something. Most commonly, the spine may need alignment, especially if your Cavalier leaps and twists in play.

Flower Essences

Flower essences, also known as Bach flower essences, are used to treat

Be alert to changes in your Cavalier's body or in his behaviour

emotional problems, such as fear of noise or shyness. Rescue Remedy, which is a mixture of five individual remedies, can be effective in cases of shock, collapse, and trauma. Many holistic veterinarians recommend this as a part of a dog's first-aid kit. Your local health food store may stock Rescue Remedy.

Herbal Medicines

When properly administered, herbal medicines may be gentler and safer than synthetic compounds, but this doesn't mean that you should give herbs indiscriminately. Natural doesn't necessarily mean safe. Follow your veterinarian's advice when it comes to using herbs.

Homeopathy

Homeopathy is based on the theory that "like heals like." A substance that normally causes the disease is diluted in several stages so that it is safe and free from side effects, yet still

Good preventive care will help to keep your Cavalier healthy and happy for years to come.

powerful enough to help in healing. Homeopathic remedies come in tablets, powders, granules, liquids, and ointments.

You know your dog better than anyone, so be alert to changes in your Cavalier's body or in his behaviour. Work in partnership with your veterinarian to help your Cavalier live a long and healthy life.

Chapter 6

Being Good

All dogs benefit from training. A Cavalier may not be much of a threat if he jumps up, and he may not be able to reach the kitchen counter to steal food, but he still should have manners. In addition, dogs are pack animals, and to a dog, his family is his pack. He expects to obey the leader, and rules help him feel secure.

The Importance of Positive Training

All dogs, no matter their size, need some training to make them a pleasure to live with. Cavaliers are no exception. Positive training methods get results and make the training easy and fun for both you and your dog. Remember the old adage "You catch more flies with honey than with vinegar." Lots of praise and tasty treats will make your dog much more eager to learn. Keep formal lessons short, and always end on a positive note, with your Cavalier doing something that he already knows how to do well.

Socialisation

Socialisation, a process in which you introduce your dog to as many new and different people, dogs, and situations as possible, isn't technically training, but it's one of the most important things you can do with your dog. Cavaliers as a breed love everyone. They think that everyone is their friend, but this doesn't mean that they don't need to get out and meet people, and with supervision, other animals. Any dog can become shy or fearful of things he doesn't understand, so it's up to you to put your puppy in different situations.

How to Socialise

Put your puppy's crate in the kitchen or the family room and let him get used to people walking by, the clatter of pots and pans, the phone ringing, and

Socialise your Cavalier to other friendly dogs.

the noise of a radio or television.

Take walks with your dog and encourage people to pat him. Sit on a bench at a shopping centre and ask passersby to give your dog a treat that you supply.

If you don't have children, make sure that he has a chance to meet some. Ask friends or neighbours, or visit a playground or park.

If you have a friend or neighbour with a friendly dog, introduce the dogs on neutral ground. Keep the dogs on lead, and make the introduction slowly. A word of caution: Supervise play with a larger dog. The dog may be friendly, but he could accidentally hurt your Cavalier if the play gets too rough. If you live near a dog park, your Cavalier can see and meet other dogs there, but be cautious about letting your dog play in a group. If there's no opportunity for your dog to meet other dogs, enrol in a puppy class. These classes are designed to help socialise your dog.

Crate Training

A crate can help to simplify training, especially housetraining. No dog likes to soil his own bed, so if you have your puppy on a reasonable schedule, he soon will learn to hold it until he is taken outside. A crate also can keep your puppy confined and out of trouble when you can't supervise him, as well as help you transport him when travelling. Don't think of a crate as a "jail." Think of it

Training Treats

Treats provide a great way to lure your dog into doing something, and those rewards help to reinforce the behaviour you want. Just remember that treats are just that—treats. They shouldn't be your dog's entire meal. Remember also that they do form part of your dog's daily calorie intake. Cut the treats up into tiny bits so that you aren't overfeeding your dog.

Soft treats work better than hard crunchy ones because your dog can chew and swallow quickly and be ready to continue working. It's also easier to get smaller pieces if the food is soft. Use a variety of foods for your rewards. Leftover chicken or steak, bits of cheese, or cooked liver are all acceptable. Or you can use commercial treats. Just remember to think small. Your dog will work just as happily for a tiny morsel as he will for a full-sized treat.

as a "den," a cosy place where your dog feels safe and secure.

How to Crate Train

To introduce your puppy to the crate, allow him to investigate with the door open. Toss a small treat into the crate. When he follows, praise him. Let him come out for another small treat. Next time, toss the treat in the crate and, when he goes to get it, close the door for about 30 seconds. Praise him and repeat again, this time for about 30 seconds longer. This is a wonderful way to build his tolerance and get him used to being in the crate gradually.

How to Housetrain

Choose a spot in your garden where you want your puppy to go. Take him to that same area every time, and bring him out on a lead so that you can direct him to the correct spot. Another reason you want your puppy on a lead is because puppies are fast, and they can get into small spaces. If you're dressed for work or school, the last thing you want to do is crawl around on your hands and knees trying to retrieve a puppy from under the hedge.

Housetraining

Housetraining is the process of teaching your dog to relieve himself outdoors or wherever else you may want him to go (like a litter box). I suppose you could just spend the entire life of your dog cleaning up after him, but your carpets would take a beating, it's likely your house would smell, and I know I'd get tired of cleaning up four or five times a day for ten years. The secret to housetraining is to have a schedule, take your puppy out frequently, be consistent, and until he is housetrained, never leave him loose unattended.

A crate is a useful tool when housetraining and travelling.

Once you get to the proper spot, encourage your puppy to go with a command. That can be any word or phrase you're comfortable with. You can say "Hurry up" or "Go potty," or "Do your business." Whatever phrase you choose, make sure that all family members use the same command. Eventually, your puppy will connect the phrase with the action.

Follow a schedule, and your puppy will soon learn to wait until he is taken out before he goes. Generally, take your puppy out after naps, after eating, and after play sessions. Carry him outside. Don't coax him to leave his crate and follow you through the house, because the odds are he won't make it, and the fewer accidents there are in the house, the faster the housetraining will go. Watch your puppy for signs that he needs to go. Some puppies will sniff and circle, but others will just squat and go, so pay attention.

If you take your puppy out for the last time around 11 p.m., he should be fine until 6 a.m. Make sure that he has a nice warm bed because if he gets cold during the night, he'll wake up, and if he wakes up, he'll need to go out. No matter where your puppy

The Expert Knows

Clicker Training

Clicker training is a popular training method that uses only positive reinforcement. Whenever your dog does something you want him to do, click and treat. The clicker marks the behaviour immediately. Your Cavalier soon learns that he gets a reward for a specific behaviour. The advantage to the clicker is that it sounds the same every time; there's never a change in volume, and a clicker never sounds impatient or angry. You can buy a clicker at most pet shops, or use the top of a ballpoint pen. If there's a trainer in your area who uses clicker training, talk to her about how to use it, or enrol in a class.

spends the day, let him sleep in a crate in someone's room so that if he does wake up, someone can take him out. Don't ignore his whining, or housetraining will take that much longer.

Paper Training

If no one is home for most of the day, and you don't have a friend or neighbour who can help, you'll need to paper train your puppy.

Confine your puppy to one room. Bathrooms, laundry rooms, and kitchens are good choices because they frequently have linoleum floors. Cover

When housetraining your Cavalier, take him outside—on a lead—to the spot where you want him to toilet.

the floor with several layers of newspapers, and put your puppy's crate, toys, and water bowl in the room. When you are home, follow a schedule of frequent trips out after naps, food, and play. When you're gone, put your puppy in the papered room. When you clean up, remove the top layers of paper, but leave the ones underneath. This will retain enough odour so that your puppy will return to that spot to go. After a week or so, reduce the area covered by the paper. If your puppy uses the paper and not the bare floor, reduce the area again. Continue until all the papers have been picked up. Don't rush this, or you'll have to start all over. Meanwhile, when you *are* home, follow a schedule of

taking your puppy outside and using a crate. Paper training generally takes longer because no one is there to praise the puppy, and the puppy needs to learn to make the transition to pottying outside. Be patient, though, and your Cavalier will learn.

Litter Training

If you live in a flat or an apartment, you may want to consider litter training your Cavalier. If that's your choice, remember to use special dog litter, not cat litter. You can train your puppy to use the litter box the same way you would train him to go outside, only instead of taking him out, you take him to the litter box. If you are paper training, put the litter box in the room with the puppy, and also spread some litter on the papers around the box. Gradually reduce the area covered by papers and litter until the puppy is left with only the litter box.

Dealing With Accidents

If your Cavalier has a housetraining accident, don't use any cleaning product that contains ammonia unless you're cleaning a litter box. Puppies follow their nose to places they've gone before, and urine contains ammonia. If your puppy smells the ammonia, he'll return to that spot. If you're using a litter box, on the other hand, this is exactly what you want him to do. Club soda works well to help prevent staining, and white vinegar helps deodorise. Oxygen-based cleaners are also very good.

Never, ever punish your puppy if he makes a mistake. Pick him up and hurry him outside. Praise him when he goes in the right place. Yelling at him after the fact does no good at all. Use patience, observation, and consistency, and you'll soon have a housetrained Cavalier.

Basic Obedience Training

You may never want to compete in formal obedience trials, and you may not care if your Cavalier ever walks in the heel position, but that doesn't mean that there aren't basics every dog should learn. Basic obedience training creates a mannerly dog who is much

FAMILY-FRIENDLY TIP

Involving Your Child in Training

Your Cavalier should obey all members of the family, so include your children in the training.

An older child might even be the primary trainer and take the dog to classes. If only one person can attend a class, make sure that person shares what she's learned so that the entire family can work with the dog. This also ensures that everyone is teaching the same way and not confusing the dog.

Even small children can be part of the training. For a treat, most dogs can be lured into a *sit* by anyone. Just remember to supervise a small child. Remind them that they aren't allowed to "train" the dog unless you are present.

more pleasant to live with than an untrained dog who is out of control.

When training your Cavalier, use lots of positive reinforcement in the form of praise and treats, and keep the training sessions short and fun. Three or four sessions of 5 minutes each are more effective than one session of 20 minutes.

Always end a session on a positive note. If you're trying to teach something and your Cavalier just isn't getting it, don't keep going. Both you and your dog will get frustrated, and that's no fun for anyone. Ask your dog to do something you know he can do, then give him a treat and lots of praise and end the session.

Sit

If your Cavalier is sitting, he isn't jumping up. Telling him to sit before you put his food dish down means that he won't jump up and knock kibble all over because he hit the bowl. And telling him to sit after he's been outside means that he won't get muddy paws on your clothes.

How to Teach Sit

Sit is one of the easiest things to teach a dog. Hold a treat in front of your dog's nose and then slowly move the treat back over the top of his head. Don't hold your hand too high, or he'll be tempted to jump up. Give the command to sit. As your hand with the treat moves back, your dog will sit as he follows the treat with his eyes and nose. The instant he sits, give him the treat and praise him.

Come

When you want your dog to come to you, the *come* command lets him know that he should show up in front of you. If it's pouring rain, and your dog is at the far end of the garden, you'll want to call him to you, not slog out to get him.

Never call your puppy if you can't reinforce the command. Train on a lead or a long line, or in a confined space with no distractions. Also, never call your puppy for something unpleasant. Call him at suppertime, but not when it's time to cut his nails. Always go and get your dog so that he doesn't associate the *come* command with something he doesn't like. When you're playing in the garden, don't just call your dog when playtime is over. Call him to you, give him a treat, and then let him

Sit *is one of the easiest commands to teach a dog.*

The Expert Knows

The Scared Dog

A dog who is afraid tries to make himself small. He will tuck his tail between his legs, drop his ears down and back (yes, even a Cavalier), and hold his head low. He also will avert his eyes. His posture says that he is not a threat.

The Anxious Dog

This same dog also may be suffering from anxiety or stress. He may be panting. A worried dog may sit with one paw raised, and he may be licking his nose, shaking himself, or yawning. A yawn briefly lowers blood pressure and helps a dog stay calm. If you notice your dog using any of these signals, try to determine what might have him worried.

The Aggressive Dog

An aggressive dog makes himself look larger. He leans forward, is up on his toes, and lifts his ears up and forward. His hackles will rise, and his tail will be up. He will stare.

The Playful Dog

Dogs use a play bow to show that they're willing to play. In a play bow, the dog lowers the front half of his body so that the forelegs are on the ground. The rear end is in the air, and the tail is wagging. The dog may give a high-pitched bark, and he may pant.

Body Language and Communication

Dogs read each other through body language, and they can read humans, too. If you stand tall and loom over a dog, that's a sign of dominance. When you lean over your dog or put your arm across his back, you are telling him that you are dominant. If you want to approach a shy or nervous dog, crouch down, turn sideways to appear smaller, and don't make eye contact. Staring at a dog is a sign of both dominance and aggression.

Your Cavalier is quickly learning your language; watch him and see if you can learn his.

go back to having fun. That way, "come" won't mean "the fun is over."

How to Teach Come

Lots of treats and a happy tone of voice should have your Cavalier scampering to you. If he's occupied with a toy or an interesting scent, call his name, say "Come," and then turn and run away. Your dog will hurry to join in the game, and then you can let him catch you and give him a treat.

Stay

Stay is a useful command that could save your dog's life. For example, if you tell your Cavalier to stay when you open the door, he won't bolt out and into the path of an oncoming car.

How to Teach Stay

Start with your dog sitting on your left. Place your open palm in front of his nose and tell him to stay. Take one step and pivot so that you are standing directly in front of the dog, then move back beside him and praise and treat. Gradually extend the amount of time you are in front of him. When he seems to understand the command, move backward a step or two. If he breaks the stay, gently replace him, repeat the command, and again step away. Don't rush this

Use a treat to reward your dog for obeying a command.

training. Be patient, and keep the lesson short and happy.

Down

Down is a way to let your dog relax in your company, and at the same time, it keeps him out of the way. A dog on a *down* can remain in a corner of the kitchen, enjoying human companionship without tripping the cook. Put your Cavalier on a *down* in the dining room, and he's not at your side, begging to share your dinner.

How to Teach Down

When teaching a dog the *down* command, many instructors will tell you to have your dog sit and then take a treat and slowly move it down toward his feet and out a bit. The dog will slide into the *down*. I've seen this work, but it's also been my experience that smaller dogs like the Cavalier tend to just pop up onto all four feet to go after the treat. If your Cavalier jumps up, keep the treat in your hand and hold your hand near the floor. He may paw or nibble at your hand, but be patient. Eventually he will lie down, at which point you can give him the treat and praise.

Walk Nicely on Lead

Your dog doesn't need to be in a formal *heel* position, but he should be able to walk on a loose lead. A dog who pulls and tugs can be more than

SENIOR DOG TIP

Techniques for Training the Older Dog

You can teach an old dog new tricks, but you may need to modify your techniques and your expectations. Keep your training sessions short, and don't expect lightning-fast responses from a senior dog. The spirit may be willing, but the flesh may be slowed down by arthritis. He may sit crookedly to accommodate a sore hip. He may come to you at a walk or a trot rather than a full-out gallop. He may not be physically able to jump through a hoop, no matter how much you want him to. An older dog also may be hard of hearing, so make sure that your dog is looking at you when you issue a command, and combine hand signals with your words.

annoying; on an icy pavement, he can be dangerous.

How to Teach Walk Nicely on Lead

The first thing to do is get your Cavalier used to the lead. Attach a light lead to his collar or harness, and let him drag it along. Never leave him unattended with the lead attached because it could catch on something. Next, pick up the end of the lead and encourage him to follow you, using treats and a happy voice. If he tries to go in another direction, stop walking. When he stops and the lead is slack, resume the walk.

Trick Training

It's always fun to teach a dog tricks, and the easiest ones to teach are those that your dog seems inclined to do anyway.

Sitting Pretty

My dog also would "sit pretty" or "beg" when I had something she really wanted, so I taught her to do it on command. Tell your dog to sit, and then move a treat back over his head, the same way you did when you taught him to sit. This time, hold it a bit higher and give your command. As soon as his front feet come off the ground, click, or praise, and treat. Soon your dog will be sitting pretty.

Jump Through a Hoop

Jumping through a hoop is easy to teach. Just remember not to ask too

A well-trained dog is a pleasure to own.

An obedience class is a great place to teach your dog basic manners.

prefer private lessons, many trainers teach both classes and private lessons.

Many local breed clubs and boarding kennels offer obedience classes. If they don't offer classes themselves, they may be able to recommend a trainer. Another source is the Association of Pet Dog Trainers (APDT).

If possible, attend a class as an observer before you enrol. Stay away from anyone who advocates hitting a dog. Look for a trainer who uses positive reinforcement. Also, pay attention to the size of the class— the larger the class, the less individual attention you and your Cavalier will receive.

much of your dog too soon. Hold the edge of a hoop on the ground and call your dog through, tempting him with a treat. When your dog is comfortable with that, raise the hoop 1 or 2 inches (2.5 or 5.1 cm) and tell your dog to jump.

How to Find an Obedience Class

An obedience class is a great place to teach your dog basic manners and get him used to other dogs and people. A class helps to keep you motivated to teach your dog because the instructor will expect progress each week. If you'd

It can be fun to teach your dog to behave, and a well-mannered dog is much more pleasant to live with. Your guests also will appreciate a dog who isn't jumping uncontrollably. Your trained Cavalier will still love everyone, but he'll do it politely.

Chapter 7

In the Doghouse

Problem behaviours may be ordinary, everyday dog behaviours, but for one reason or another, they've gotten out of hand. Barking, for instance, is normal behaviour for a dog, but a dog who barks nonstop when left alone may disturb the neighbours. Digging the occasional hole as a puppy may be overlooked, but if your adult dog is turning your back garden into something resembling Swiss cheese, then the digging is a problem. When a small dog jumps up, he may be easier to pet, but he also may be leaving muddy paw prints on good clothes, and a dog suffering from separation anxiety may start to chew furniture into kindling.

epending on the problem, a veterinary exam may be in order. If your Cavalier has always asked to go out but is now going to the bathroom indoors, there may be a physical reason. Once you are sure that your dog is healthy, you can take steps to eliminate the problem behaviour. Other problem behaviours arise because the dog is bored. He wants something to do, so he digs a hole, barks, or chews on a chair leg. A tired dog is a good dog, so make sure that your Cavalier gets enough exercise.

Keep in mind that it's easier to stop a habit from forming than it is to correct that habit once it's established. If you don't intend to allow your adult dog on the furniture, for example, don't let the puppy snuggle with you on the sofa. Your dog will be confused, and he won't understand why the rules change when he grows up.

Make sure that all the members of the family know the rules. It's important to be consistent with your dog. If Dad says no jumping but Mom and the kids encourage it, your Cavalier won't know what he's supposed to do.

Be consistent with what you allow your Cavalier to get away with, such as sitting on the furniture.

Toy Dogs and Problem Behaviours

The biggest mistake owners of toy dogs make is forgetting that their pet is a dog. It's so easy just to pick up a toy dog that sometimes the dog never walks anywhere. A dog who is always cuddled and pampered may growl at the approach of strangers. Instead of correcting the behaviour, owners of toys sometimes pet and comfort the dog. That just reinforces the nasty behaviour. It isn't cute if a 100-pound (45.4-kg) dog growls and snaps, and it isn't cute if your 15-pound (6.8-kg) Cavalier does it either. Treat your dog like a dog and expect proper behaviour.

Everyone should be speaking the same language, too. For example, use "down" to mean "lie down" and "off" to mean "don't jump." It doesn't matter what word you use, as long as everyone uses the same word.

Now let's take a look at some common canine problem behaviours.

Barking

Dogs bark for a variety of reasons, but it's important to remember that barking is a natural doggy behaviour—excessive barking is the real problem. Fortunately, Cavaliers are not known for excessive barking.

Solution

If your dog is barking out of boredom, make sure that you never leave him out in the garden unattended for long periods of time. If he starts to bark, bring him in immediately. If your dog is barking at people passing by or a neighbour's

dog, consider installing a solid fence, or plant shrubs to screen the pavement or the neighbour's garden. Dogs rarely bark at things they can't see. Supply interesting toys, or better yet, play with your dog yourself. It will give him exercise, stop him from barking, and he'll love being with you.

A dog who barks constantly when

To prevent unwanted chewing, give your dog an appropriate chew toy.

he's home alone may be barking because he's anxious. This can take a long time to correct, so be patient. Start by leaving the house. Close the door, then re-enter your home almost instantly. Praise your dog and give him a treat. Leave again, and count to five. Go back in. Praise him and give him a treat. Don't rush the process. The goal is to be able to leave and return without your dog barking. Work up to longer and longer periods of time until your dog no longer barks when you're not around. Eventually he will realise that you aren't leaving him forever. You also can try giving your dog a toy that dispenses treats as it's played with, or get a hard rubber toy that has a space for peanut butter or cheese. These toys give your dog something to do instead of think about how much he misses you.

Consider teaching your Cavalier to bark on command. Once he knows that command, you can teach him to stop. When your dog barks, praise him for "speaking" and give him a

treat. Eventually, he'll connect the command to speak with barking. Now, teach him to stop. The minute he stops, say "Quiet" or whatever command you've chosen, and give him a treat. I've found that combining a hand signal with the *quiet* command helped my dog learn this more quickly. I kept the treats in my clenched fist, and when I raised my fist and said "Quiet!", he knew there was a treat coming and stopped barking.

You can use this same system to get your dog to stop barking when you answer the door. Get a friend to help, and have her ring the bell or knock on the door. Only open the door when your dog has obeyed the *quiet* command. Have your friend give your dog a treat. In time, he will learn that he can bark at the door, but when it opens, he should be quiet.

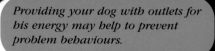

Providing your dog with outlets for his energy may help to prevent problem behaviours.

Chewing

Chewing is what dogs do for recreation. Chewing on the proper item can help to clean the teeth, and dogs enjoy it immensely. Puppies, especially, will chew on anything and everything. Part of that is exploratory. They are learning about their world, and like a human toddler, they need to put everything into their mouths. When a puppy starts teething, he chews to soothe his itchy gums. It's up to you to make sure that what your dog chews is acceptable to you.

Solution

First, keep your clothing and shoes out of reach. There's nothing nicer in a dog's mind than a nice leather loafer or a sock that smells wonderful, at least to him! Give your Cavalier lots of appropriate chew toys. If he's teething, wet an old hand towel, tie several knots in it, and freeze it, then give it to him to gnaw on. The cold will feel good on those sore gums. (Supervise this chewing session so that your dog doesn't swallow clumps of towel, or you'll have another problem on your hands.)

If your dog is still heading for the leg of the dining room chair, crate him when you're not home to watch him. There are also products that you can buy to put on objects that give them a bitter taste and supposedly discourage your dog from chewing them. Sometimes this works, and sometimes

Finding a Behaviourist

A professional trainer can help many dog problem behaviours, but there may come a time when you need an animal behaviourist. The best place to start your search is by asking your veterinarian for a referral. Members of your local breed club also may be a good source of information. There is no national standard for certification as an animal behaviourist, so consider credentials and ask for references. If you can't find a behaviourist locally, check out the website for the Association of Pet Behaviour Counsellors at www.apbc.org.uk.
It's unlikely that you'll ever need this level of help with your Cavalier, but if you do have a problem, don't hesitate to get professional help. The earlier you do, the more likely the problem can be solved.

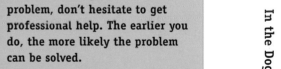

the dog just ignores the bitterness because it's too much fun to chew. If your dog goes after that chair when you see him, distract him with a toy or a game. If you catch him chewing it, tell him no and trade him for something that's acceptable to chew.

Older dogs enjoy chewing, too.

Finding the Lost Dog

If your dog should become lost, don't rely on tags, tattoos, or microchips to get him back. All those things may help, and your dog should have some form of identification, but there's more you can do. Make up posters and put them on area notice boards, in veterinarians' surgeries, and at local shops. The posters should include a picture of your dog, so keep a good photo on hand in case you need it. The photo should show your dog clearly. If he is dark, use a light background, and vice versa. If the photo is black and white, list the colour or colours of your dog. Don't say "Blenheim" or "tri-colour." Say "brown and white," or "black, white, and brown." Remember, not everyone will be familiar with Cavaliers. List your phone number and the area where the dog was lost. Mention your dog's sex, as well as age, although it may be more helpful to say "puppy" or "older dog." If your dog was wearing a collar, mention that. Offer a reward, but don't specify the amount on the poster.

Go door to door and ask neighbours if they've seen your dog. Talk to children. They may cover more territory on foot than adults. Ask children to come to you or to tell their parents if they think they see your dog. Discourage them from trying to catch your dog. Even a gentle dog may snap or bite when frightened.

Call local veterinary hospitals in case your dog has been hit by a car and taken to a veterinarian. Call again. Check your local animal shelter. Go in person and look at the dogs. Don't rely on phone calls, and don't depend on someone from a shelter calling you. Leave your name and number by all means, but also check in person. Notes can be lost, and personnel may change. Your dog may be at the shelter, but the workers may not realise that he's a Cavalier. Go look at the dogs at least every other day, and show the shelter staff a picture of your dog.

Run an ad in the lost and found column of your local newspaper. Ask your area radio stations to announce it as well. Many newspapers and radio stations will run this type of announcement as a public service at no charge.

Nylon bones are a good choice, as are hard rubber toys, especially if they're the kind you can fill with peanut butter or cheese. Rawhide chews are another choice, but again, supervise. Some dogs have no problem at all with rawhide, but others will chew off chunks and swallow them. These chunks can turn into an indigestible lump in the stomach. The bones made from shredded, compacted rawhide don't last as long, but there is no danger of the dog swallowing huge pieces.

If you want to give your dog an occasional real bone, make sure that it is fresh and uncooked. Cooked bones can be harmful. Supervise the chewing session, and after a day or two, discard the bone. The older the bone, the more it dries out, which means that it becomes like a cooked bone, more apt to splinter and pose a danger to your dog should he swallow those splinters.

Digging

Puppies of any breed may dig a hole or two, but if your adult Cavalier is digging craters in your garden, think about why and use those reasons to help you formulate a solution to the problem.

Solution

Sometimes dogs dig because they're warm, and lying in cool dirt feels good. If this is the case with your dog, make sure that he has access to shade and isn't left outdoors too long.

Cavaliers are very people-oriented,

FAMILY-FRIENDLY TIP

Children and Doggy Problem Behaviours

Cavaliers are a loving breed, but any dog can exhibit problem behaviours, and depending on the behaviour, there may not be a safe way for your child to interact with the dog. A Cavalier could jump up and bite a child's face faster than you could stop it. Don't take that chance. Even dogs without a problem never should be left alone with very small children.

so maybe he's digging out of boredom. Supply toys, and play with him yourself to discourage digging.

It could be that your dog just enjoys digging. Cavaliers aren't known for digging the way terriers are, but every dog is an individual. If your dog just seems to enjoy it, consider giving him his own sandbox. Mark off an area of the garden with a low frame of wood or plastic, and either fill it with sand or dig up the soil. Lightly bury a few smelly treats, and praise him when he digs them up. Bury a couple of treats every day until he understands that that's his own special spot for digging.

In the Doghouse

Housetraining Problems

Some dogs who seemed to be housetrained suddenly start relieving themselves indoors, just as they did when they were puppies. This can occur for a variety of reasons, including sudden changes in their potty schedule, too much freedom in the house, and normal incontinence that can be attributed to ageing.

Solution

First, schedule an appointment with your vet to rule out any physical problems. Once you've ruled out a medical condition, then you can try some other solutions.

Dogs are creatures of habit. Has your pattern of when you let him out changed? If he's always gone out at noon, and now you don't get home until 2:00 p.m., he may just be going at his regular time.

If there haven't been any major changes in lifestyle, maybe you've just given your dog too much freedom in the house too soon. Back up to basic housetraining. Crate your dog when you're not home. Follow a routine, just as you did when your dog was a puppy.

Is your dog a senior? Seniors can be perfectly healthy but still need to go out more often. If you've adopted an older dog who is housetrained, he may just be confused and anxious in his new environment. Many well-

Keep your dog from jumping up by teaching him an alternative behaviour, such as sit.

trained dogs will relieve themselves indoors if they're stressed. Go slow, and start at the beginning. Make certain rooms off limits until you can trust your dog. Take him out on a regular schedule, and crate him when you can't watch him. If the dog is used to a crate, this will be a good way to help calm him as well. That cosy, den-like feeling of the crate will make him feel safe and secure.

Jumping Up

It's hard to get angry at a small dog who jumps up. Many small dogs jump up because they want to get closer to their owners, and Cavaliers don't weigh much, so they're unlikely to knock you over. A dog who jumps up is also easier to pet, so sometimes people allow the behaviour for that reason. There are times, though, when you may not want to encourage this behaviour. If you have small children, even a tiny dog can knock them off balance. The same goes for an older person who may not be steady on her feet. Or your dog may frequently have muddy paws, and even if you don't mind the jumping behaviour, your visitors might.

Solution

Recruit your friends for this training. Anytime your Cavalier jumps up, turn

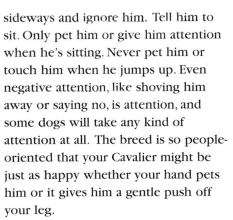

The Expert Knows

Aggression and Separation Anxiety

You may be able to alleviate separation anxiety yourself by giving your dog exercise before he's left alone so that he's tired, and also by leaving him with toys that make him work to get a treat reward. If these tips don't work and your dog is destructive, it may be time to talk to a professional. If your dog is aggressive, start with a thorough veterinary exam to rule out any physical cause for the aggression. If your dog is fine physically but is aggressive, don't try to deal with the problem yourself. Contact a professional immediately.

sideways and ignore him. Tell him to sit. Only pet him or give him attention when he's sitting. Never pet him or touch him when he jumps up. Even negative attention, like shoving him away or saying no, is attention, and some dogs will take any kind of attention at all. The breed is so people-oriented that your Cavalier might be just as happy whether your hand pets him or it gives him a gentle push off your leg.

If you would like your dog to jump up sometimes, teach him a command, such as *hup* or *jump* or *hug*. That way, he'll only jump when you want him to

SENIOR DOG TIP

Training the Senior With a Problem Behaviour

Dogs are creatures of habit, so it's much harder to break a habit than it is to teach them the proper behaviour in the first place. That's not to say that it can't be done, but you'll need to be patient and consistent. For example, if your dog has always slept on the sofa, but now you don't want him to, distract him every time he is on the sofa. Offer a treat or a game. Guide him to the bed you want him to use, and give him lots of praise and treats every time he goes to his bed. When you're not around, block access to the sofa so that he is never allowed to use it as a bed.

If the habit is more threatening, you may need a professional trainer or a behaviourist. For example, if you've allowed your dog to nip at your ankles, and that nip is getting harder and it's no longer a game, call a professional.

and not when his paws are muddy. Pat your leg and tempt him with a treat. Give your command. It won't be long before your Cavalier understands.

Nipping

All puppies learn from their mother and siblings not to bite too hard when playing. If, for some reason, your puppy didn't learn this lesson, it's up to you to teach him that nipping people is unacceptable.

Solution

If your puppy is nipping your hands in play, yell "Ouch!" and stop the game. He soon will learn that biting too hard ends the fun. Your puppy also may nip at ankles if you or a child is running.

Cavaliers aren't a herding breed, so

there's not that instinctive urge to chase and nip, but some dogs will chase anything moving. If that happens, again, yell "Ouch!" and stop moving to end the game.

Any dog can be teased beyond his limit and snap to protect himself. Make sure that no one is teasing your dog or backing him into a corner where he feels trapped and needs to defend himself.

Cavaliers are generally sweet and loving, so if an older dog starts nipping or snapping, schedule an exam with your veterinarian. Your dog may have a physical problem. It may hurt him to be touched or picked up, and he may be snapping because he's in pain. If there's no physical cause for the nipping, you may need to consult a behaviourist.

Cavaliers are typically a quiet, loving breed, but individuals can exhibit problem behaviours. Be firm and consistent as you train your dog, and if there's a problem you can't correct yourself, don't hesitate to seek professional advice. Don't let things get out of hand before you call for help, either—it's much easier to correct a problem while it's small. Once the problem is solved, you can look forward to many happy years with your loving Cavalier.

If your dog jumps up, a professional trainer can help.

Chapter 8

Stepping Out

If Cavaliers had a job description, it would be "stay close to the family." Cavaliers are real people lovers, and as a result, they love doing anything as long as they're with you, from showing in conformation to competing in performance events to riding along when you run errands. With a little training, you can take your Cavalier just about anywhere.

Travel

Travel is always more fun when the entire family can go, and with a little advance planning, your dog can join the fun.

What to Pack

If you plan to travel with your dog, plan to pack for him as well. He won't need a suitcase full of clothes, but he will need some basics:

Collar or harness with ID tags. Make sure that your dog is wearing a collar or harness with ID tags, even if he has a microchip. You may want to make up an extra tag that includes the phone number of the place where you'll be staying.

Crate. If your dog travels on the seat, secured by the seat belt, take along a crate for hotel room stays. If your dog travels in a crate, you can either take that crate into the hotel room or carry an extra for the room. Lightweight folding models don't take up much room and are easy to set up.

First-aid kit. Pack a doggy first-aid kit, and include your dog's vaccination records. If you are travelling overseas you will need your pet passport.

Nonbreakable food and water dishes are best when travelling.

Food and water dishes. Nonbreakable food and water dishes are best for a trip. You even can buy folding dishes, or for food, use paper plates and there won't be any dishes to wash.

Food and water. Carry enough of your dog's food and water for the trip. Even if your dog loves to travel, it's still stressful, and a change in food or water can lead to digestive upsets. Don't assume that your brand of dog food will be available everywhere. If you'll only be gone two or three days, carry all the water your dog will need. If the trip will be longer, gradually replace water as you use it so that your dog can get used to the change gradually.

Lead. Your regular lead is fine for travelling, although some people like to use a retractable lead to give their dog more exercise and freedom. If that's your choice, be aware of other dogs and people in the area so that your Cavalier doesn't approach unfriendly dogs or people who don't like, or are afraid of, dogs.

Medications. Take any medications your dog may be on, including flea and tick treatments.

Sheet. Carry along an extra sheet for the hotel room bed if you plan to let your Cavalier join you on the bed. Bedspreads aren't laundered between guests, and dog hairs can work their way into the fabric. If you don't want to carry your own sheet, ask housekeeping at the hotel to provide an extra for you.

Towels. Carry along extra towels. Towels can serve as bedding for your dog, and if he gets muddy or wet, you'll need towels for that as well. Pack paper towels and plastic bags for cleanup as well.

Toys. Take a favourite toy or two; your dog will appreciate something familiar.

If you will be spending more than a day or two at your final destination, get the name and number of a veterinarian or emergency clinic in the area. That way, if there's a problem, you won't waste valuable time trying to locate a veterinarian.

Car Travel

If your trip will be by car, make sure that your Cavalier is used to car rides. Take short, happy trips, even if it's just down the road. Make sure that every ride doesn't end at the veterinarian's. How eager would you be to get in the car if you always got a shot at the end of the ride?

Don't let your dog ride loose in the car. Pop him into a crate, or invest in a harness that connects to a seat belt. Make sure that your dog is always in the back seat area as well. Front-seat air bags can seriously injure or kill a small dog.

Travelling with your Cavalier will help to cement your bond.

SENIOR DOG TIP
Travelling With the Older Dog

Older dogs love to be included in family activities, especially a Cavalier, who considers it his job to stay close to his people. Your dog will love to travel with you, but keep in mind that older dogs need more frequent rest stops. An older dog may stiffen up more during a long ride, or he may have arthritis, so don't let him leap from the car when you stop for a rest. Help him from the car. Help him into the car, too, if he's having trouble making the jump.

It's even more important for an older dog to have the food and water he's used to. The older your dog gets, the less change his digestive system will be able to handle. As with any dog, if your senior is on medication, make sure that you have enough to last for the entire trip.

Once you've arrived at your destination, remember that your dog isn't as spry as he once was. He may want to go on that hike with you, but physically, it may be too much for him. Take a pleasant short walk with him, and then let him snooze in your room while you conquer that mountain trail.

Never leave your dog in a closed car, especially in warm weather. Even on a cool or overcast day, the temperature in a closed car can reach lethal levels. Keep in mind, too, that shade is no guarantee that your dog will be safe. Shade moves, and that shady spot may be in direct sun in an hour or two.

Airline Travel

If you're flying to your destination and your dog will be in the cargo hold, remember that airlines won't fly a dog if the temperature will be below 45°F (7.2°C) or above 85°F (29.4°C) any place where the plane lands. Some airlines also limit the number of animals they will fly. If your Cavalier will fit into a soft-sided carrier, he should fit under the seat, but there seems to be less and less room under those seats. Check with your airline well ahead of your trip for their rules and regulations. If your dog is flying as cargo, and you don't see him being loaded, have the counter agent call the ramp to make sure that your dog is on board. It's not going to be a good vacation if you're in Edinburgh and your dog is in Manchester. At your destination, go to the pick-up area immediately. If your dog hasn't been unloaded, you'll want to know that before the plane takes off again.

If you decide to fly with your Cavalier, resist the temptation to give him a tranquiliscr. Short-nosed dogs may have difficulty breathing, and a tranquiliser is going to compound the problem.

Finding Pet-Friendly Lodging

Don't trust luck when you're travelling with a dog. You may very well find a hotel that accepts dogs, or you may find yourself driving late into the night because, at every place you stop, you're welcome but your dog is not.

There are several books on the market that give details of places that will accept your dog. For example, Pets Welcome.

Another option is to go online and check out specific hotel chains. You may discover that all hotels in a particular chain accept dogs, or that a chain refuses dogs. Some hotels base acceptance on the weight of the dog, which shouldn't be a problem with a Cavalier.

Some hotels make their decisions on whether or not the dog will be crated or has had obedience lessons. However you go about finding a dog-friendly place, it's a good idea to call

ahead and make a reservation. Some hotels have a certain number of dog rooms, and once those are booked, they will turn you away. Another good reason to call is that policies change. That charming hotel that greeted your Cavalier with open arms last year may now have a "no dogs allowed" sign.

Competitive Sports

Competitive sports are a great way to spend time with your Cavalier, and they

FAMILY-FRIENDLY TIP

Travelling With Your Dog and Child

Your child will love having the company of a dog on a long trip, and having the dog along may even cut down on the number of times you hear the phrase "Are we there yet?" If your dog travels in a crate, give your child the job of making sure that the dog is comfortable. Have her check the water bowl periodically. Carry snacks that appeal to both child and dog. Carrot sticks and apple slices, for instance, can be shared.

When travelling with both children and dogs, try to stop for a rest every two or three hours.

give your dog something to do that uses both his brain and his body. Win or lose, you'll both have fun!

Agility

Agility is one of the most popular performance events, and as well as being fun, it gives both you and your Cavalier exercise. The idea is to complete the course in the fastest time possible with the fewest number of errors. Most agility courses include a tunnel, an A-frame, a teeter-totter, a pause table, and weave poles. Just remember to make sure that your Cavalier is fully mature before competing so that he doesn't damage growing bones or put stress on unformed joints.

Conformation (Dog Shows)

If your Cavalier is "show quality"—that is, he fits the written standard of the breed, with no major faults—you might want to show him in a dog show. Dogs in conformation compete for Challenge Certificates. If a dog wins three Challenge Certificates under three separate judges, it is entitled to be known as a Champion.

Many breed clubs offer handling classes, and these classes are an excellent way to learn how to handle your Cavalier in the show ring.

Agility courses contain a variety of obstacles, such as the tunnel.

Conformation events evaluate dogs against their breed's standard.

Cavaliers are a "table" breed, which means that the judge examines the dog on a grooming table. Your dog will need to learn to stand quietly on the table while the judge runs her hands over him and checks his teeth. Get your dog used to having his mouth opened. Your dog also will need to trot at your left side so that the judge can watch his movement. Handlers get their dogs' attention and teach them to stand, or "stack," by giving them treats. In the show ring, the treats are called "bait." The bait is usually liver, but it can be anything your dog loves, as long as he eats it quickly.

A match is an informal event run just like a dog show. Participating in a match is a good way to practice before you enter a real show. The entry fees at matches are much less than for a show, and the setting is more casual.

Flyball

If your Cavalier likes to retrieve, he might enjoy flyball. Flyball is a relay race in which each dog on the team leaps over four hurdles, hits a pedal that releases a tennis ball, catches the ball, and returns over the hurdles.

Obedience

Obedience is a sport in which you and your dog execute a standard set of commands issued by a judge, including heeling, sitting, lying down, staying, recalling, retrieving, and jumping. You may not talk to your dog except to give commands, and points are deducted for repeat commands. Obedience has several levels, from pre-beginner through to Class C.

Rally Obedience

Rally obedience, a sport found mainly in the US, is similar to obedience, but it is less formal. You can give multiple commands, and you can talk to your dog as much as you like. It's a good way to see if you'll enjoy obedience. Depending on the level of competition, 10 to 20 stations are set up in a rally course. At each station, a card lists instructions, such as "down" or "stand for examination." Once you complete the exercise, you move on to the next station.

Tracking

Tracking tests your dog's ability to follow a scent. Different levels of competition vary in difficulty, depending on the length of the track, how many turns there are, and whether you have to go over or around obstacles.

Noncompetitive Activities

If you want to have fun with your dog,

The Expert Knows

Sports and Safety

Just like human athletes, your dog must be in good physical condition to compete in dog sports. Exercise with him, and condition him with practice sessions. Before you compete, stretch your dog and warm him up. After competition, allow him to cool down, and give him water. Cavaliers don't have the short muzzles of Pugs or Bulldogs, but their faces are still short, so they can overheat faster than longer-muzzled breeds. Cavaliers take a long time to mature—sometimes two or three years. For this reason, never train heavily until your dog is at least 18 months old. For the first year of your Cavalier's life, limit jumping, and don't jog or run long distances or you could damage growth plates in bones or injure a joint that is not fully formed.

but you don't want to compete, there are lots of noncompetitive ways that you and your Cavalier can have fun.

"101 Things to Do with a Box"

If you're clicker training your dog, try this game, which was developed by clicker guru Karen Pryor: See how many things you can get your dog to do with an ordinary cardboard box, from shoving it with his nose to jumping inside it to tipping it over.

Hide-and-Seek

Put your dog on a *sit-stay*, and run and hide. Call him to see how long it takes him to find you.

Hide the Treat

Invert three plastic bowls, and hide a treat under one of them. Tell your dog to find the treat. Or hide a treat in a room and have your dog find it. Place the treat someplace obvious at first, and then increase the difficulty as your dog catches on.

Several books on the market provide information on formal competitions and informal tricks and games you can enjoy with your dog. The key word is "enjoy." Have fun with your dog, whether it's a game of hide-and-seek or an agility trial. The more time you spend with your Cavalier, the happier you'll both be.

Tracking tests a dog's ability to follow a scent.

Resources

Associations and Organisations

Breed Clubs

The Kennel Club
1 Clarges Street
London
W1J 8AB
Telephone: 0870 606 6750
Fax: 0207 518 1058
www.the-kennel-club.org.uk

American Kennel Club (AKC)
5580 Centerview Drive
Raleigh, NC 27606
Telephone: (919) 233-9767
E-mail: info@akc.org
www.akc.org

Canadian Kennel Club (CKC)
89 Skyway Avenue, Suite 100
Etobicoke, Ontario M9W 6R4
Telephone: (416) 675-5511
E-mail: information@ckc.ca
www.ckc.ca

Federation Cynologique Internationale (FCI)
Secretariat General de la FCI
Place Albert 1er, 13
B – 6530 Thuin
Belqique
www.fci.be

United Kennel Club (UKC)
100 E. Kilgore Road
Kalamazoo, MI 49002-5584
Telephone: (269) 343-9020
E-mail: pbickell@ukcdogs.com
www.ukcdogs.com

The Cavalier King Charles Spaniel Club
www.thecavalierclub.co.uk

The Scottish Cavalier King Charles
Spaniel Club
wwww.cavaliers.co.uk

Pet Sitters

National Association of Registered Pet Sitters
www.dogsit.com

UK Petsitters
Telephone: 01902 41789
www.ukpetsitter.com

Dog Services UK
www.dogservices.co.uk

Rescue Organisations and Animal Welfare Groups

Royal Society for the Prevention of Cruelty to Animals (RSPCA)
Telephone: 0870 3335 999
Fax: 0870 7530 284
www.rspca.org.uk

Scottish Society for the Prevention of Cruelty to Animals (SSPCA)
Braehead Mains
603 Queensferry Road
Edinburgh EH4 6EA
Telephone: 0131 339 0222
Email: enquiries@scottishspca.org
www.scottishspca.org

Cavalier King Charles Spaniels

British Veterinary Association Animal
Welfare Foundation (BVA AWF)
7 Mansfield Street
London W1G 9NA
Telephone: 0207 636 6541
Email: bva-awf@bva.co.uk
www.bva-awf.org.uk

Sports

Agility Club UK
www.agilityclub.co.uk

International Agility Link (IAL)
Global Administrator: Steve Drinkwater
E-mail: yunde@powerup.au
www.agilityclick.com

British Flyball Association
PO Box 109
Petersfield GU32 1XZ
Telephone: 01753 620110
Email: bfa@flyball.org.uk
www.flyball.org.uk

Therapy

Pets As Therapy
3 Grange Farm Cottages
Wyombe Road, Saunderton
Princes Risborough
Bucks HP27 9NS
Telephone: 0870 977 0003
www.petsastherapy.org

Therapy Dogs International (TDI)
88 Bartley Road
Flanders, NJ 07836
Telephone: (973) 252 7171
Email: tdi@gti.net
www.tdi-dog.org

Training and Behaviour

Association of Pet Dog Trainers (APDT)
PO Box 17
Kempsford GL7 4W7
www.apdt.co.uk

Association of Pet Behaviour Counsellors
PO Box 46
Worcester WR8 9YS
Telephone: 01386 751151
Email: info@apbc.org.uk
www.apbc.org.uk

British Institute of Professional Dog Trainers
www.bipdt.net

Veterinary and Health Resources

British Veterinary Association (BVA)
7 Mansfield Street
London
W1G 9NQ
Telephone: 020 7636 6541
Fax: 020 7436 2970
E-mail: bvahq@bva.co.uk
www.bva.co.uk

British Veterinary Hospitals Association (BHVA)
Station Bungalow
Main Road, Stockfield
Northumberland NE43 7HJ
Telephone: 07966 901619
Email: office@bvha.org.uk
www.BVHA.org.uk

Royal College of Veterinary Surgeons (RCVS)
Belgravia House
62-64 Horseferry Road
London SW1P 2AF
Telephone: 0207 222 2001
Email: admin@rcvs.org.uk
www.rcvs.org.uk

British Small Animal Veterinary Association (BSAVA)
Woodrow House
1 Telford Way, Waterwells Business Park
Guedgley
Gloucester GL2 2AB
Telephone: 01452 726700
Email: customerservices@bsava.com
www.bsava.com

British Association of Veterinary Opthalmologists (BAVO)
Email: hjf@vetspecialists.co.uk
Email: secretary"bravo.org.uk
www.bravo.org.uk

British Association of Homeopathic Veterinary Surgeons (BAHVS)
Alternative Beterinary Medicine Centre
Chinham House
Stanford in the Vale
Oxfordshire SN7 8NQ
Email: enquiries@bahvs.com
www.bahvs.com

Association of Chartered Physiotherapists Specialising in Animal Therapy (ACPAT)
52 Littleham Road
Exmouth, Devon EX8 2QJ
Telephone: 01395 270648
www.acpat.org.uk

Association of British Veterinary Acupuncturists (ABVA)
66A Easthorp, Southwell
Nottinghamshire NG25 0HZ
www.abva.co.uk

Publications

Books

Nester, Mary Ann
Agility Dog Training
Interpet Publishing, 2007

Harvey, Su
Good Pup, Good Dog
Interpet Publishing, 2007

Evans, J M
What If My Dog?
Interpet Publishing, 2006

Tennant, Colin
Mini Encyclopedia of Dog Training & Behaviour
Interpet Publishing, 2005

Barnes, Julia
Living With a Rescued Dog
Interpet Publishing, 2004

Evans, J M & White, Kay
Doglopaedia
Ringpress Books, 1998

Evans, J M
Book of the Bitch
Ringpress Books 1998

Anderson, Teoti
The Super Simple Guide to Housetraining.
TFH Publications, 2004.

Morgan, Diane
Good Dogkeeping
TFH Publications, 2005.

Magazines

Dog World Ltd
Somerfield House
Wotton Road, Ashford
Kent TN23 6LW
Telephone: 01233 621877

Dogs Today
Town Mill, Bagshot Road
Chobham, Surrey GU24 8BZ
Telephone: 01276 858880
Email:
enquiries@dogstodaymagazine.co.uk
www.dogstodaymagazine.co.uk

Kennel Gazette
Kennel Club
1 Clarges Street
London W1J 8AB
Telephone: 0870 6066750
www.thekennelclub.co.uk

K9 Magazine
21 High Street
Warsop, Nottinghamshire NG20 0AA
Telephone: 0870 011 4114
Email: mail@k9magazine.com
www.k9magazine.com

Our Dogs
Our Dogs Publishing
5 Oxford Road, Station Approach,
Manchester M60 1SX
www.ourdogs.co.uk

Your Dog
Roebuck House, 33 Broad Street
Stamford, Loncolnshire PE9 1RB
Telephone: 01780 766199

Dogs Monthly
Ascot House
High Street, Ascot,
Berkshire SL5 7JG
United Kingdom
Telephone: 0870 730 8433
E-mail: admin@rtc-associates.frccserve.co.uk
www.corsini.co.uk/dogsmonthly

Index

Note: **Boldfaced** numbers indicate illustrations.

Cavalier King Charles Spaniels

Cavalier King Charles Spaniels

111

Index

Dedication

For Sonny Paxson, a very special Cavalier.
In memory of Darcy Thornton.

Acknowledgments

Thanks to Kelley Adair, Robin Olsen, and Darlene Wahlstrom.

About the Author

Susan M. Ewing has been "in dogs" since 1977. She owned and operated a boarding kennel and enjoys showing and participating in various performance events. She is affiliated with the Dog Writers Association of America and the Cat Writers' Association. Since 1964, Susan has been writing professionally for newspapers, magazines, and radio. She writes a weekly column, "The Pet Pen," for The Post-Journal (Jamestown, NY). She currently lives in Jamestown, New York, with her husband, Jim, and two dogs.

Photo Credits

André Klaassen (Shutterstock): 4, 61, 82, 94
N Joy Neish (Shutterstock): front cover photo, 9, 68
Jeff Thrower (WebThrower) (Shutterstock): 11
All other photos courtesy of T.F.H. archives and Isabelle Francais.